Vika Kirchenbauer

Compassion
and Inconvenience

Vika Kirchenbauer

Preface

Everything that today appears self-evident once came into being. What today seems normal about artists and art exhibitions becomes complicated when considered against a neglected context of origin: the first public presentations of contemporary art in mid-18th century London, which were inextricably entangled with early capitalism and British colonialism. At that time, how, for whom and under what conditions contemporary art enters the public sphere was defined by a small circle of white men—and with lasting effect. One birthplace of the contemporary art institution turns out to be the Foundling Hospital,[1] a care facility for "deserted young children", in which private economic and colonial interests intersected with notions of charity and practices of refinement. In subsequent developments, moral philosophical concepts and artists' feelings—most distinctly around compassion and inconvenience—played a role in inserting dominance and imaginings of superiority into the core of European notions of art and taste.

This reader combines the two main outcomes of my engagement with this historical context: the 30-minute video work *Compassion and Inconvenience* (2024)—its script is reproduced alongside stills and audio descriptions; and my essay *Instituting Inconvenience and Colonial Relations: The Genesis of European Contemporary Art Institutions in Mid-18th Century London* (2025).[2]

Much of the research for the project would not have been possible without the generosity of archivists, most notably Mark Pomeroy at the Royal Academy of Arts Archives, and Eve Wilson at the Royal Society of Arts Archives. I would also like to thank Alison Duke at the Foundling Museum, as well as Caitlin Kennedy and Carol Homden at Coram. Further thanks are extended to the Braunschweig University of Art for supporting this publication, and to Mousse Publishing for including it in their programme. Thank you to Anna Azzali for the great design, and to Nancy Chapple and Rosie Heinrich for copy editing. For lending their brilliance to *Compassion and Inconvenience*, I am deeply grateful to the performers Laurie Young, Mmakgosi Kgabi, Olympia Bukkakis, Leah Marojević and Lauren John Joseph. I am equally indebted to the wonderful crew who contributed their talents to the video's production:

[1]
The Foundling Hospital continues today as the children's charity Coram.

[2]
The essay was originally commissioned by Tamara Antonijević and Christopher Weickenmeier for the reader *Assistances: On Reproductive Labour in the Arts* published by b_books, where the same text appears in parallel.

Rita Macedo, Azadeh Zandieh, Jay Barry Matthews, Alexis Mersmann and Sarah Hartgens. My most profound gratitude goes to Judith Sieber, who drew my attention to this historic constellation, and whose sharpness immeasurably enriched both the video work and the essay.

Vika Kirchenbauer

Instituting Inconvenience and Colonial Relations:

The Genesis of European Contemporary Art Institutions in Mid-18th Century London

From today's perspective, the French revolutionary government's opening of the Louvre in 1793—with a collection of 537 paintings—is generally regarded as the birth of the national art museum. Art historians widely concur that "[t]he French Revolution created the first truly modern art museum when it designated the Louvre museum a national museum",[1] and that "[t]he Louvre [...] is usually and correctly identified as the archetypal state museum and model for subsequent national art museums the world over."[2] The transformation of the Louvre from a royal palace to a public museum highlights a significant moment in the democratisation of culture, as the French Revolution effectively turned confiscated royal and church property into collective property. Admission was free, and the general public was invited into what was now declared a public institution. Artists, who were to regard the institution as a main point of reference, were even offered special days to visit the museum.[3] Up to today, the emergence of the national art museum from an anti-aristocratic revolution serves as an emancipatory narrative that, with its radiance, often stands in for the institutionalisation of art at large.

In his much-quoted *The Birth of the Museum*, sociologist Tony Bennett asserts, in reference to art historians Carol Duncan and Alan Wallach, that the early objectives of the Louvre were "to make a new conception of the state visible to the inspection of the citizen".[4] In post-revolutionary France, the impressive display of art inside the Louvre signalled to the public that power and national wealth had shifted from the crown to the state. At the same time as the state legitimised itself through the public exhibition, it redefined the visitor, who was no longer addressed as a subordinate, but as a citizen.[5] Feminist scholars like Duncan and Elke Krasny make sure to add that this birth of the museum was tethered to an idea of male citizenship and to a conception of a public sphere from which women were explicitly excluded.[6] These critical engagements highlight how the Louvre was closely entangled with the interests of the nation, and also reproductive of contemporary gender realities.

Rooted in this constellation set out in the Louvre, academic and artistic critique has frequently focused on the pursuit of hegemonic interests through public art institutions. These perspectives are influenced by established critical approaches that assess museums as instruments of social control and discipline. While the

[1] Carol Duncan, 'Art Museums and the Ritual of Citizenship', in *Exhibiting Cultures: The Poetics and Politics of Museum Display*, edited by Ivan Karp and Steven D. Lavine (Washington and London: The Smithsonian Institution Press in association with the American Association of Museums, 1991), p. 88.

[2] Andrew McClellan, *Inventing the Louvre. Art, Politics, and the Origins of the Modern Museum in Eighteenth-Century Paris* (Berkeley: University of California Press, 1994), p. 2.

[3] Within the ten-day week implemented in post-revolutionary France, artists were allowed inside the Louvre for the first six days of the week, the general public for the next three days, and the last day of the week was reserved for repairs.

[4] Tony Bennett, *The Birth of the Museum: History, Theory, Politics* (London: Routledge, 1995), p. 38.

[5] See Carol Duncan and Alan Wallach, 'The Universal Survey. Museum', *Art History 3* (December, 1980), p. 456.

points of critique take aim at the institutionalisation of art, faith is usually kept in the overall emancipatory and democratising principles ascribed to art itself, and the artist comprehended as a subversive figure. Within this line of thinking, the artist is framed as a visitor to the institution, who upon professional engagement becomes a shareholder in it. The artist's agency is complicated as soon as they enter into a relationship with the institution, which, to think with Marina Vishmidt's term, then serves as a "phantom antagonist".[7] Different waves of institutional critique have therefore framed the artist as becoming complicit with or representative of the institution and its relations at the moment of their inclusion.

These assumed relations between artist and institutional "phantom antagonist" as separate entities, however, are inconsistent with how contemporary art institutions really came about. As it turns out, the allure of the story of the Louvre has overshadowed a neglected context of origin that needs to be taken into account. If the Louvre's public exhibition of the formerly royal collection made it the first state art museum, then the first privately-sponsored contemporary art institution has its roots in an unlikely place: in a care facility for "deserted young children". Half a century before the opening of the Louvre as a public museum, in mid-18th century London, contemporary British artists exhibited their works to the wealthy patrons of the Foundling Hospital [FIG. 1], a children's home in which private economic and colonial interests intersected with notions of benevolence and the pursuit of refinement. Viewed from today, this narration is uneasy and challenging to identify with: artists do not assume an emancipatory role, but establish methods of exclusion to lasting effect. After showing their works in the Foundling Hospital, the same group of artists set out to gain broader recognition and fame, organising the first public exhibitions of contemporary art in central London, and finally founding the Royal Academy of Arts in 1768. Their actions in this particular context reveal the contemporary art institution as a manifestation of artists' desires, or, more concretely, as the instituted outcome of an emerging white male artistic elite who sought to protect their work from the poor, and who strove to inscribe themselves into a new upper middle class.

In this essay, I will explore these first public exhibitions, as well as the episodes and circumstances

6

See Elke Krasny, 'Citizenship and the Museum: On Feminist Acts', in *Feminism and Museums: Intervention, Disruption, and Change*, edited by Jenna Ashton (Edinburgh and Boston: MuseumsEtc, 2017), pp. 74–99; Carol Duncan, *Civilizing Rituals: Inside Public Art Museums* (London: Routledge, 1995).

7

Marina Vishmidt, 'Between Not Everything and Not Nothing: Cuts Toward Infrastructural Critique' in *Former West: Art and the Contemporary After 1989*, edited by Maria Hlavajova and Simon Sheikh (Cambridge, Massachusetts: The MIT Press, 2017), pp. 265–69.

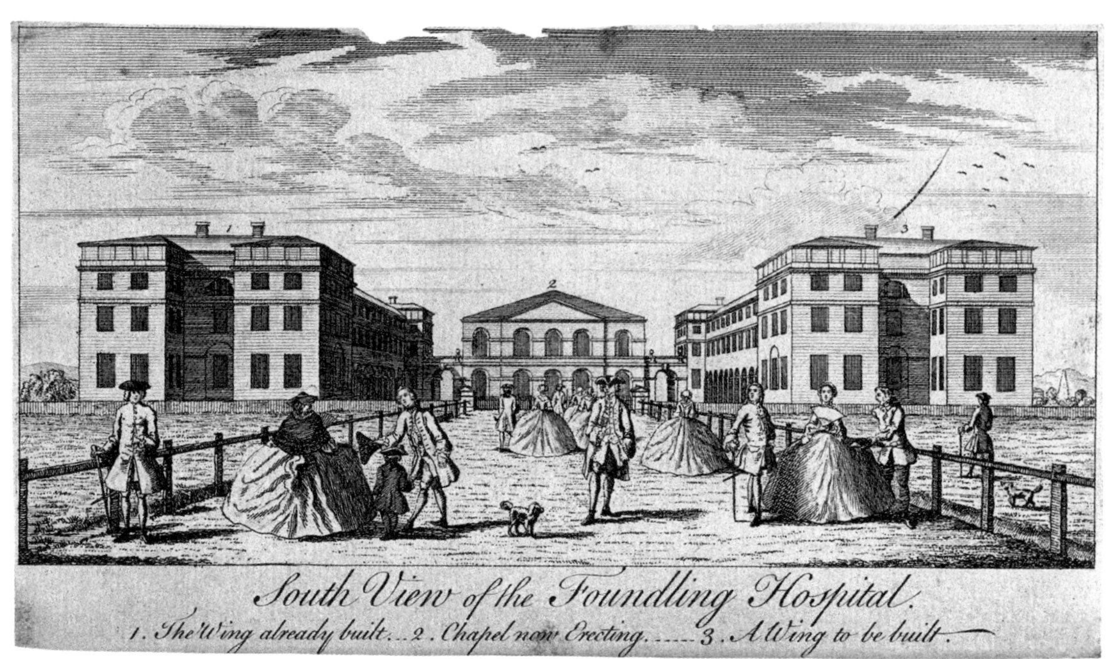

FIG. 1
South View of the Foundling Hospital, Lamb's Conduit Field, London, 1748. Engraving, 9.9 × 19.6 cm.
Wellcome Collection

leading up to them, as the historical genesis against which
to re-examine what today seems self-evident about artists
and institutional exhibitions of contemporary art. To this
end, I will trace prevailing conceptions of art to their
ideological and material interconnectedness with ideas
from Liberalism and the Scottish Enlightenment as well
as with British colonialism. The Foundling Hospital was
conceived as a privately-sponsored institution, and is
a product of crucial transformations taking place in
regard to cultural practices, public sentiments and colonial relations. Therefore, before focusing on its foundation
and the resulting art presentations more closely, it will
be necessary to situate these developments within the
political, social, philosophical and art-theoretical context
of the time.

This British model from the 18th century of
relying primarily upon private citizens to establish art
institutions historically became the standard in many
countries, most prominently the United States. And while
it is true that many major museums and art institutions,
especially in continental Europe, do come from royal,
church or state legacies, the reality now is usually more
complex. After decades of neoliberal policymaking, most
of today's cultural institutions are now de facto joint
ventures, in which private economic and reputational
concerns routinely intermingle with state interests and
budgets.[8] These current workings of art closely resonate
with the first public exhibitions of contemporary art
and their political implications. A closer look at this
historical scene produces important questions not only
about the continuities of institutionalised exclusions
and forms of violence, but also about the ways in which
artists' self-conceptions, as well as their feelings and
desires relating to taste, patronage and admission fees,
are enmeshed in them.

[8] For an insightful account, see Karen Archey, *After Institutions* (Berlin: Floating Opera Press, 2022), pp. 17–23.

ART HELPS PEOPLE FROM THE MIDDLE-CLASS RISE

As Britain intensified its colonial efforts in the early
18th century, dispossession, enslavement and exploitation provided the grounds upon which industrialisation
would later emerge. The unequal nature of colonial
trade permitted some members of the commercial
classes, who were part of the middle classes at the time,
to acquire wealth to extents previously only conceivable

for the members of the upper classes, such as nobility or aristocracy. A possibility of social mobility was introduced in which, according to postcolonial scholar Simon Gikandi's insightful study *Slavery and the Culture of Taste*, "birthright and rank were no longer considered to be the golden standards in determining modes of behaviour or social relationships."[9] Instead, taste and politeness, concepts in which art assumed a defining role, testified to a person's character and resolved their position within a changing concept of citizenry. These transformations upset the rigid system based on lineage and titles. To consume or even support culture, however, money was needed, which made economic success a prerequisite to participation in polite culture. Hence, this new form of social mobility—though measured in terms of proximity to art and culture—was ultimately based on the pursuit of economic advantage. A core function of the culture that emerged around notions of taste was accordingly also "to harmonize commerce and virtue".[10] Within this culture, art did not serve as a refined cover for unvirtuous or impolite trade. Instead, the proximity of commerce and art presented them as part of the same polite project. Economic expansion and the acquisition of wealth were viewed as expressive of cultural refinement.

This development "coincided with a rise of the status of the painter from a skilled executor of commissions to a person (almost always a man) who could operate with more ambitious social or aesthetic ideas [...]."[11] Up until that moment, the social status of artists had traditionally been low. Although artists usually came from families of middle-class professionals, which afforded them the general education required to converse with their aristocratic patrons, they had little presence in the spaces of public life. Their work was regarded as a craft, and most artists specialised in specific genres, such as portrait, landscape or history painting, that were ordered hierarchically. Now, however, a new conception of the artist was constituted, as not merely someone trained in apprenticeships to produce art in a skilful manner, but as someone whose complex cultural contributions served as discursive references in various fields of knowledge production. The production of paintings in particular was elevated from being considered a mere job to a serious affair.[12] As Gikandi notes, "[a] key component of the modernising gesture of European culture in the

[9] Simon Gikandi, *Slavery and the Culture of Taste* (Princeton: Princeton University Press, 2011), p. 18.

[10] Ibid., p. 115.

[11] Brandon Taylor, *Art for the Nation: Exhibitions and the London Public, 1747–2001* (Manchester: Manchester University Press, 1999), p. 2.

[12] Ibid.

eighteenth century was the location of art at the center of systems of knowledge."[13]

Taste linked the public to the figure of the artist, through whom objects for the development of taste materialised. The learning of taste was more than a matter of "good breeding" or of internalising what to like; it was a form of expertise that required deep engagement with the arts as part of a liberal education that gave access to various discursive renderings. Leisure time, or time for education, were luxuries that people in lower social positions were not granted access to. This turned hobbies and interests such as art into widely recognised status symbols.[14]

Previously, connoisseurship and the possession of art were the preserve of the aristocracy, who built collections in country houses, accessible only to members —usually men—of the same social rank. Rarefication and exclusivity were central to these private displays of art, which provided no place for the public, and consisted primarily of so-called Old Masters. The commercial classes' interests in relation to art, in contrast, were different. They envisioned the public to serve as a witness to their ascension, testifying that refinement, taste and politeness could be acquired—just like wealth. Consequently, it was of great interest to the commercial classes that their prestige become publicly visible. In addition, many of the wealthier members of the commercial classes were also eager to distinguish themselves from other less economically successful or ostensibly less cultured members of their own class. Art collecting therefore served a double purpose: it stood as evidence of a person's advantage over other individuals, and also enabled the commercial classes to measure themselves against the aristocracy. The underlying struggle was related to the question of who, in the future, might constitute the ruling class.

The artists at the time understood that the commercial classes' ascent to leading positions within British society would be aided through their support of British art. In contrast to the aristocracy's focus on the so-called Old Masters, usually imported from the European continent, the emergence of a new, contemporary school of national art would support the British Empire's claims to higher civilisation and superiority over the rest of the world, and, in turn, allow the commercial classes to act as patrons of the country's cultural status. Naturally, the most renowned artists pictured themselves to be at

[13] Simon Gikandi, *Slavery and the Culture of Taste* (2011), p. 12.

[14] See Hugh Cunningham, *Time, Work and Leisure: Life Changes in England since 1700* (Manchester: Manchester University Press, 2014).

the forefront of such a new contemporary British school of painting. They were interested in being recognised as professionals of gentlemanly status, and their situation was such that they were dependent on patronage. So far, both had been difficult to attain, since they had nowhere to exhibit, and their studios were often too shabby to welcome wealthy clients or supporters. This motivated the artists to form societies and clubs to promote their interests and to emphasise that these interests overlapped with those of other stakeholders, since, evidently, this historical situation bore the potential of being advantageous for several parties: the artists, the nation and the commercial classes.

15 See Catherine Hall, *Civilising Subjects: Colony and Metropole in the English Imagination, 1830–1867* (Chicago: University of Chicago Press, 2002), pp. 16–17.

16 Simon Gikandi, *Slavery and the Culture of Taste* (2011), p. 16.

RATIONALISING CATEGORIES OF DIFFERENCE

The time of the British Empire is when categories of difference were being elaborated across the lines of class, race and gender.[15] The rationalisation of these categories was closely related to culture and produced through notions of taste. While gentlemen were framed as the custodians of taste, "[w]omen, slaves, and the poor [...] were deployed in a subliminal, subordinate, or suppressed relation to the culture of taste."[16] If the study of art became a means through which taste could be acquired and refinement could be exercised, this attributed a civilising function to art. Once this civilising quality of art was established, notions of beauty and taste developed into distinguishing markers between those who were recognised as civilised and those who were not.

Philosophers of the time contributed to the development and legitimisation of these new power structures and social relationships. Despite its uninspiring and perhaps misleading title, *A Treatise on Ancient Painting* by Scottish philosopher and theologian George Turnbull from 1740 offers crucial insights into the ways in which contemporary art in the 18th century developed into a social and cultural differentiator. The recourse to antiquity, as undertaken by Turnbull, and in particular to the Roman Empire, was a common means at the time of presenting the British Empire as a new rendition of the same dominance. At the centre of Turnbull's reasoning, however, is the reconciliation of moral philosophy with the theory of painting, on which he builds his concept of moral works of art that are intended to move the viewer. Moving the viewer, in this context, should be read in a double sense, both emotionally and socially: Turnbull discusses moral works of art as defined by their capability to touch the viewer's social sentiments, a process that, in turn, is proclaimed to morally raise the same viewer above others. He discusses art as elevating humanity into the rational, dignified and graceful spheres, away from the bodily joys identified as part of the animal world:

What is it that gives either Grace, or Dignity, or Relish to human Life, but the ingenious Arts? What else is it that raises Society to true Grandeur? Take away the Virtues and Arts, and what remains but merely sensual and animal Gratifications? What remains that is peculiar to Man, that exalts him above the groveling Brutes, or intitles [sic] a Society of Men to the Character of a Rational Society?[17]

"The Virtues and Arts", portrayed as two wings of the same dignifying project, are postulated as distinguishing features between moral practices and "merely sensual and animal Gratifications". This defines a polite and moral self in contrast to a devalued other, the rational in opposition to the sensual. The "true Grandeur" achieved through the arts is presented as defining "man", as that which "exalts him above the groveling Brutes". This makes exercises of refinement synonymous with the possession of humanity. Art therefore played an important role within the theoretical underpinnings of the question of who belongs in the category of the human.

LIBERAL UNIVERSALISM AND COLONIAL RELATIONS

Liberalism propagated universal principles, while at the same time reinforcing the categories of difference that for many people turned liberalist ideals such as freedom and equality into their opposites. This occurred not least because this liberal universalism succeeded in abstracting a very specific circumstance and position into a normative standard. The categories of difference that were established and rationalised in the 18th century through culture, art and philosophy were anchored in their time and locality, yet purported general legitimacy irrespective of political or cultural context. This is to say that European concepts that were imposed as universal were derived from very specific schools

[17] George Turnbull, *A Treatise on Ancient Painting, Containing Observations on the Rise, Progress, and Decline of that Art amongst the Greeks and Romans; The High Opinion which the Great Men of Antiquity had of it; its Connexion with Poetry and Philosophy; and the Use that may be made of it in Education* (London: Printed for the author, and sold by A. Millar, 1740), p. 122.

of thought and historical trajectories, a circumstance that conflicts with any assertion of universal validity. In addition, these concepts also originated from particular subject positions, generally those of a white men of class privilege. Tying universalist thought back to its specific local socio-political context therefore means questioning how the general and abstract ideas of Liberalism and the European Enlightenment related to place, gender, class and race.

With regard to the British context, it becomes clear that the arts served an important function in universalising specific notions of taste and aesthetics as normative standards. The "advancement of grandeur and elegance" served to underpin claims to superiority, instrumental not only within the class stratification of a nation, but also in regard to its global status. And if aesthetics and their appreciation were to be a measure for a country's or a person's position in relation to others, a universal standard was deemed necessary. The "man of affluence", rather than the state, the church or the crown, was assigned a defining role in providing such a standard through his "desire of excellence". In the introduction to *London and Westminster Improved, Illustrated by Plans to which is prefixed, A Discourse on Publick Magnificence* [FIG. 2], published in 1766, architect John Gwynn notes:

Let us consider the man of affluence, actuated by that beneficent spirit, the mere delight of doing good, and rendering himself acceptable to his Creator; he is furnished with the means, and by employing the ingenious and laborious artizans, adds to the necessity of labour, the desire of excellence: A villa rises, an estate is improved, and a manufacture established; these create the proper distinction between the Prince and the peasant, the merchant and the workman; these characterize the genius of a nation, mark the æra of its excellence, raise it from obscurity to fame, and fix it as the standard of taste to latest posterity.
[...]
Our wisdom is respected, our laws are envied, and our dominions are spread over a large part of the globe. Let us, therefore, no longer neglect to enjoy our superiority; let us employ our riches in the encouragement of ingenious labour, by promoting the advancement of grandeur and elegance.[18]

In this instance, what serves to distinguish between social classes within a society, also serves to distinguish between

John Gwynn, *London and Westminster Improved, Illustrated by Plans to which is prefixed, A Discourse on Publick Magnificence, with Observations on the State of Arts and Artists in this Kingdom, wherein the Study of the Polite Arts is recommended as Necessary to a Liberal Education* (London: 1766), pp. xiv–xv.

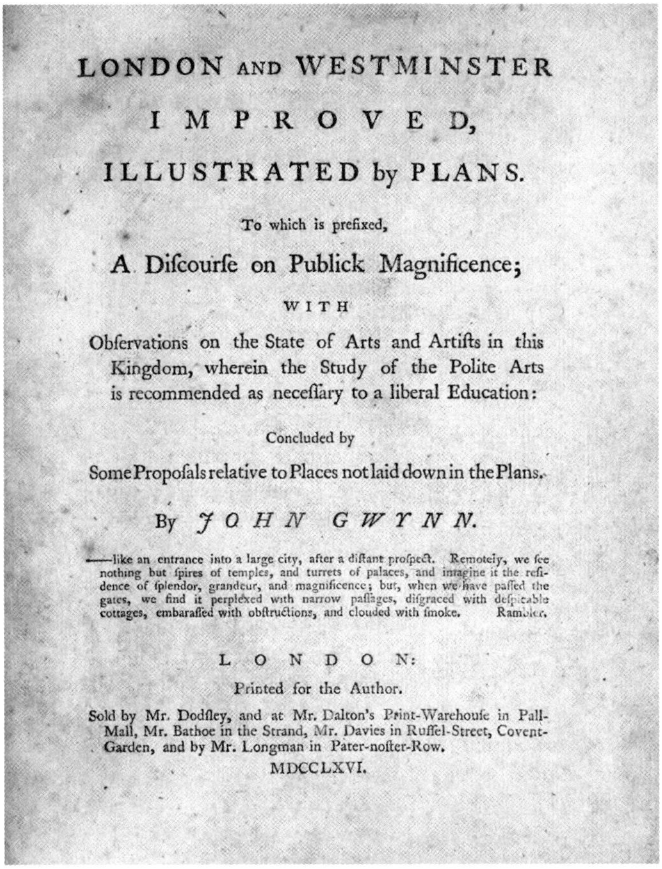

LONDON and WESTMINSTER IMPROVED,

ILLUSTRATED by PLANS.

To which is prefixed,

A Difcourfe on Publick Magnificence;

WITH

Obfervations on the State of Arts and Artifts in this Kingdom, wherein the Study of the Polite Arts is recommended as neceffary to a liberal Education:

Concluded by

Some Propofals relative to Places not laid down in the Plans.

By *JOHN GWYNN.*

——like an entrance into a large city, after a diftant profpect. Remotely, we fee nothing but fpires of temples, and turrets of palaces, and imagine it the refidence of fplendor, grandeur, and magnificence; but, when we have paffed the gates, we find it perplexed with narrow paffages, difgraced with defpicable cottages, embaraffed with obftructions, and clouded with fmoke. *Rambler.*

LONDON:

Printed for the Author.

Sold by Mr. Dodfley, and at Mr. Dalton's Print-Warehoufe in Pall-Mall, Mr. Bathoe in the Strand, Mr. Davies in Ruffel-Street, Covent-Garden, and by Mr. Longman in Pater-nofter-Row.

MDCCLXVI.

FIG. 2
John Gwynn, *London and Westminster Improved, Illustrated by Plans to which is prefixed, A Discourse on Publick Magnificence, with Observations on the State of Arts and Artists in this Kingdom, wherein the Study of the Polite Arts is recommended as Necessary to a Liberal Education* (London: 1766). Wellcome Collection

the supposedly different levels of civilisation of countries. To fix a nation "as the standard of taste to latest
posterity", as Gwynn puts it, means first to universalise
notions of taste as general principles, and then to set
the standard once and for all within these principles.
A specific moment, in which many European nations
intensified their colonial expansion, was identified as an
opportunity to establish a lasting order by hierarchising
notions of taste. This resonates closely with what Scottish
Enlightenment philosopher David Hume writes in his
essay "Of the Standard of Taste", published roughly
a decade before Gwynn:

*Thus though the principles of taste be universal, and nearly,
if not entirely the same in all men; yet few are qualified to give
judgment on any work of art, or establish their own sentiment
as the standard of beauty.*[19]

Rather than allowing different forms of aesthetic appreciation to exist according to their own principles, Hume
argues for a general validity of the principles of taste.
Inconsistent responses to phenomena would therein be
measured against a single standard. Taste is proclaimed
as universal, applying to everybody the same, regardless
of locality and context. To claim that "the principles of
taste" exist in "all men" is to suggest that everybody is,
in theory, capable of appreciating beauty in (nearly) the
same manner. Humans, globally, are dragged into the
same set of rules, and accepted as equal in principle only,
but not in actuality. That's because despite the principal
rules applying to all, only some are considered qualified
to set the standard. This notion becomes particularly
enlightening if read in conjunction with what is added
only a few pages later:

*Though men of delicate taste are rare, they are easily to be
distinguished in society, by the soundness of their understanding
and the superiority of their faculties above the rest of mankind.*[20]

According to Hume, rare men of "delicate taste"—
coincidently white and European—are in possession of
superior "faculties above the rest of mankind." These
distinguished men, elevated over "the rest of mankind"
through their taste, are thus legitimised to "establish
their own sentiment as the standard of beauty." Taste
and appreciation of beauty did not, therefore, stand in

[19] David Hume, 'Of the Standard of Taste', in *Four Dissertations* (London: A. Millar, 1757), p. 228.

[20] Ibid., p. 231.

opposition to colonial violence; on the contrary, they were its ideological basis and thus a necessary prerequisite. Within colonial constellations, European notions of taste assumed a foundational role in justifying the subjugation and exploitation of people and nations all over the globe.

In regard to the British Empire's trade relations with Africa, in his *Commercial and Political Atlas* from 1786, Scottish political economist William Playfair[21] admits that "[t]he nature of this trade [is] certainly not the most honourable in the world."[22] He goes on to vindicate it, however, by describing goods of no value to Europeans as "suited to the taste" of those receiving them in exchange for humans, gold and ivory:

[T]he Africans receive the most rascally articles that the ingenuity of Europeans has found means to produce. In return for our fellow creatures, for gold, and for ivory, we exchange the basest of those articles that are suited to the taste or the fancy of a despicable set of Barbarians.[23]

In what follows, Playfair describes how "the ingenuity of deceit found out a way of making" bracelets supposedly consisting entirely of brass instead "of cast iron, [...] and covering them with a solution of copper, which sold for brass."[24] In Playfair's assertion it is implied that only refined taste and connoisseurship allow a person to judge the value of an object. The deception described is therefore portrayed not as an unvirtuous act, but as a sign of "ingenuity" that reflects superiority. Not only is aesthetic judgment thereby measured against universalised European notions of taste, it is also conflated with a judgment of trade value, which presupposes all societies to act according to the same capitalist logic as it originated in Europe. *Manillas*, as these bracelets are referred to, were cheaply produced, often in the same European factories that also produced chains and bolts used for enslavement,[25] and became the first general-purpose money in West Africa, where they were also a principal currency in the trade of enslaved people.[26]

COLONIALISM FUNDS THE ARTS

The triangular trade was at the heart of Britain's economic progress and the originating catalyst for capitalism and the Industrial Revolution, as Caribbean historian and

[21]
For an intriguing study on the emergence of the timeline, which deals extensively with Playfair's trade charts, see Judith Sieber, *Die Erfindung des Zeitstrahls: Eine Kritik der Sichtbarmachung von Zeit und Handel im 18. Jahrhundert* (Bielefeld: Transcript Publishing, 2025).

[22]
William Playfair, *The Commercial and Political Atlas; Representing, by Means of Stained Copper-Plate Charts, the Exports, Imports, and General Trade of England; the National Debt, and Other Public Accounts; With Observations and Remarks. To Which are Added, Charts of the Revenue and debts of Ireland* (London: J. Debrett, 1786), p. 89.

[23]
Ibid.

[24]
Ibid., p. 90.

[25]
See Gail Cameron and Stan Crooke, *Liverpool: Capital of the Slave Trade* (Liverpool: Picton Press, 1992).

[26]
See Jane I. Guyer and Karin Pallaver, 'Money and Currency in African History', in *Oxford Research Encyclopaedia of African History*, edited by Thomas Spear (New York: Oxford University Press, 2018), pp. 1–28.

later politician Eric Williams argues in his groundbreaking study *Capitalism and Slavery*, from 1944.[27] As Williams describes, the profits from slavery represented the principal source for the accumulation of capital in Britain. This influx also changed the faces of cities in the 18th century. Contemporary artists were aware that the proliferation of expensive architecture across Europe was financed by colonial wealth. This is exemplified in *A Dialogue on Taste*, published by Scottish painter Allan Ramsay in 1762. Two characters, Philomathes and Misopapistes, discuss the concept of taste and its importance in society, noting that the "[i]ncrease of trade and riches, all over Europe, particularly from the new-discovered Indies, produced a great number of sumptuous buildings in the new fashion; so that the fondness for it [...] grew, in a little time, to be a real taste or sentiment."[28]

In the 18th century, private capital derived from slavery was habitually transformed into symbols of refinement, setting standards for the tastes and cultural practices of an elite. Artists, in turn, solicited the patronage of these elites, or offered their services to them. That colonialism and the wealth it generated were identified as an opportunity to raise the social status of the arts on a broader level is evident in Gwynn's *London and Westminster Improved*, in which he presents architectural plans for the urban renewal of London, and advocates the study of the "polite arts" as integral to a liberal education. In the book's introduction, he describes art as a natural development resulting from settler-colonial expansion and subsequent refinement. Gwynn narrates the emergence of art and architecture as part of a chain of causal events: once "a colony of emigrants" has satisfied its own needs, commerce and navigation are introduced; subsequently "wealth arises, and [...] the rich inhabitants look out for the means of ease, pleasure and distinction; these produce the polite arts, and the original formation of huts is now converted into architecture; painting and sculpture contribute to the decoration, and stamp that value on canvas and marble which is acknowledged by taste and discernment and mark those necessary distinctions between the palace and the cottage."[29]

This linear narration of supposed progress presents the project of empire as productive of the "polite arts", and as its necessary precondition. The economic self-interest of the "rich inhabitants," who are at the forefront of imperial expansion, forms the basis for their

[27] See Eric Williams, *Capitalism and Slavery* (Richmond: The University of North Carolina Press, 1944).

[28] Allan Ramsay, *A Dialogue on Taste* (London: 1762 second edition, 1755 first edition), p. 47.

[29] John Gwynn, *London and Westminster Improved* (1766), pp. xiii–xiv.

support of the arts. This reflects the reality of the time, when it was mainly people who belonged to a "colony of emigrants" who played a defining role in funding art. The most important patrons of cultural production were not, in fact, the British commercial classes who benefited from colonial trade as merchants, but colonial barons who resided overseas.[30] Art historian and novelist David Dabydeen points out that "in the eighteenth century the term patron still had a dual meaning of 'owner of slaves' and 'supporter of the arts', for some of the outstanding connoisseurs and collectors of the age were heavily involved in the slave trade."[31]

SUGAR-COATING: WHITE INNOCENCE

Sugar planters were some of the richest business people, and consequently also art's most important patrons. Those operating further from the British polite sphere, on the supposed margins of the empire, were particularly committed to charity and the advancement of the arts. Colonial barons had reputational interests in being closely connected to tasteful and refined spheres, even at a distance. As polite gentlemen capable of appreciating art, and as disinterested and charitable philanthropists, they could refashion themselves as incapable of cruelty. Their support of the arts therefore fundamentally served to sustain what, in another context, cultural historian Saidiya Hartman has phrased as "the ignorance and the innocence of the white world."[32] Philanthropy was a useful means of nurturing an attachment to a form of innocence necessarily anchored in disavowal.

Sugar was not only closely connected to the funding of art's production; it was also central to many of the routines of polite culture in 18th-century London. Members of the commercial classes met in coffee houses, where colonial products were consumed. Here, sugar served as "the commodity that sweetened the pivot of coffee around which the culture of taste revolved."[33] Coffee houses, however, were also sites for trade, of art but also of enslaved people. [34, 35] The sensorial tasting of colonial goods and the acquisition of fine cultural taste were intimately connected, and both depended on exploitation and the ignorance thereof. The craving for sweetness—which to Europeans was the taste of virtuous leisure—created a demand for sugar, thus becoming

[30] See Simon Gikandi, *Slavery and the Culture of Taste* (2011), p. 111.

[31] David Dabydeen, 'Blacks and the Polite World of Eighteenth-Century English Art', *Kunapipi* 6(2) (1984), p. 45.

[32] Saidiya Hartman, *Lose Your Mother: A Journey Along the Atlantic Slave Route* (New York: Farrar, Straus and Giroux, 2007), p. 169.

[33] Simon Gikandi, *Slavery and the Culture of Taste* (2011), p. 109.

[34] For instance, the sale by auction of "[a] fine Collection of Pictures by some of the best Italian, French, Flemish, Dutch, and English Masters" at John's Coffee-house in Sheer Lane is advertised in *The Daily Post*, Friday 7 April, 1727.

[35] Examples of the sale of enslaved people in coffee houses—with the earliest instance being from 1708—can be found in Bryant Lillywhite, *London Coffee Houses* (London: G. Allen and Unwin, 1963), pp. 86, 190.

a main catalyst for the triangular trade.[36] As Williams emphasises, "[i]n the nineteenth century no less than in the eighteenth Britain's ambitious plan was to become the sugar emporium of the world [...]."[37] The new identities that were being fashioned in Britain around refinement and social virtues were based on the brutality of enslavement and the violence on the plantations, where sugar was associated not with sweetness but with forced labour. On the interconnectedness of colonial exploitation with notions of politeness and high culture, Dabydeen notes that "[t]he eighteenth century was indeed a period in which the High Civilization of England and the Barbarity of the Colonies were literally, two sides of the same coin."[38]

A RETIRED SEA CAPTAIN AND ABANDONED CHILDREN

In the second quarter of the 18th century, a series of privately sponsored hospitals emerged in London that privatised care and education.[39] The term hospital was used broadly, referring not only to medical institutions, but also to organisations such as charity schools for poor children or retirement homes for sailors. These organisations were considered more efficient than the parish-based administration of poor relief, and generally followed the model of joint-stock companies, a forerunner of the modern corporation.[40] Mostly funded by the commercial classes, these hospitals enabled "the largely unenfranchised bourgeoisie to play a part in the formulation and pursuit of national programmes conducive to their own interests."[41]

Traditionally, the care of the poor had been the responsibility of the parishes. In 1723, however, important transformations came about when the Poor Relief Act was passed with the objective of reducing the demand for poor relief. The law introduced the idea that the poor could be turned productive, and allowed parishes to establish workhouses. Only those who were desperate enough to accept the conditions of hard labour in the workhouses remained entitled to poor relief. The possibilities of what could be produced in these workhouses aroused the interest of the commercial classes. They considered high death rates, however, especially amongst the poor, an obstacle to making better use of this part of the population. Especially child mortality rates at

[36] See Simon Gikandi, *Slavery and the Culture of Taste* (2011), p. 110; James Walvin, *Fruits of Empire: Exotic Produce and British Taste, 1660–1800* (Basingstoke, UK: Macmillan, 1997), pp. 122–23; Eric Williams, *Capitalism and Slavery* (1944), p. 23.

[37] Eric Williams, *Capitalism and Slavery* (1944), pp. 163–64.

[38] David Dabydeen, 'Blacks and the Polite World of Eighteenth-Century English Art' (1984), p. 47.

[39] See Donna T. Andrew, *Philanthropy and Police: London Charity in the Eighteenth Century* (Princeton: Princeton University Press, 1989), pp. 17–34.

[40] See David H. Solkin, *Painting for Money: The Visual Arts and the Public Sphere in Eighteenth-Century England* (New Haven: Published for the Paul Mellon Centre for Studies in British Art by Yale University Press, 1993), p. 158.

[41] Ibid.

the time were extremely high. As the so-called "bills of mortality" printed weekly in the newspapers show, around 75 percent of children in London died before the age of five between 1730 and 1749.[42] According to contemporary sources, such as philanthropist and social reformer Jonas Hanway, the death rate of children was even higher in workhouses.[43] The tremendous loss of life constituted an immediate threat to imperial expansion and consequently to the maintenance and advancement of private wealth. Amongst the commercial classes there was concern that the country could run out of personnel necessary for its survival. Soldiers were needed for the continental wars Britain was involved in, overseas trade and colonial projects produced a demand for sailors, and maids and labourers were sought for work in households and manufactures. The funding of hospitals was therefore an investment conducive to the commercial classes' scheme of increasing the nation's population.

In the 1720s, Thomas Coram [FIG. 3], a retired captain and shipwright who had been active in the American colonies, began to seek support for his plan to erect a hospital for abandoned children. Under the impression of "the shocking Spectacles he had seen of innocent Children who had been murdered and thrown upon Dunghills",[44] he drafted a first petition to King George II, soliciting a Royal Charter for the establishment of such a charity. One major obstacle the petition faced in the contemporary climate was public morality around children considered illegitimate. A common suspicion was that the existence of an institution that housed, clothed and nurtured children would encourage reckless sexual behaviour amongst the poor. To counteract this criticism and to give the project an air of respectability, support from aristocratic women was pursued. After the petition received its first signature in 1729 by Charlotte Finch, Duchess of Somerset, it took six more years of campaigning until a further twenty women of rank also added their names. The petition opens with expressions of "Compassion for the Sufferings and lamentable Condition of such poor abandon'd helpless Infants", and argues that a charity as proposed would "supply the Government plentifully with useful Hands on many Occasions" and "better produc[e] good and faithful Servants from amongst the poor and miserable, cast-off Children or Foundlings". This focus on compassion and a prospect to usefulness contrasts with the verdict

[42] M. Dorothy George, *London Life in the Eighteenth Century* (Harmondsworth: Penguin, 1966 third edition; 1925 first edition), p. 39; see also 'Abstract of the London Weekly Bill' in *The London Magazine* (London: 1732), p. 319.

[43] Jonas Hanway, *An Earnest Appeal for the Mercy to the Children of the Poor* (London: Sold by J. Dodsley, in Pall-Mall, 1766), p. 50.

[44] *An Account of the Methods which have been used for the Establishment of an Hospital for the Maintenance and Education of Exposed and Deserted Young Children*, 1749 (The London Archives, A/FH/A/01/005/001, from Coram's Foundling Hospital Archives), p. iii.

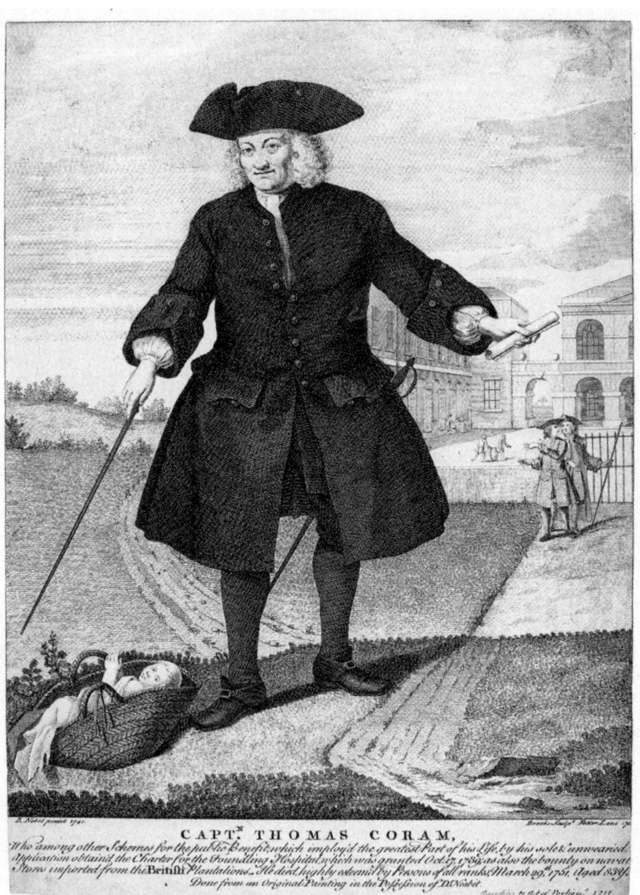

FIG. 3
J. Brooke after Balthasar Nebot, *Portrait of Thomas Coram*, 1751. Line engraving, 12 × 16.5 cm. Wellcome Collection

expressed in the same letter that the children were "a Pest to the Publick, and a chargeable Nuisance within the Bills of Mortality".[45]

As can be seen in Coram's petition, the objects at which supposedly generous sentiments like pity and compassion are directed, are, simultaneously, degraded and devalued. Compassion thus framed is represented as a complex emotion that needs triggering through other emotions like disgust or fascination, which are not mutually exclusive. To be disgusted or engaged by someone else's suffering can serve as the basis for accessing compassion. This points to an affective constellation that will prove to be a defining feature of the polite commercial classes' relation to other people's misery. Within this setup, compassion and degradation are intricately intertwined, and those inspiring compassionate responses are simultaneously perceived as inconvenient.

Concern and insult also go hand in hand in a pamphlet from 1728 by clergyman Thomas Bray, a friend of Coram's, who likewise promotes the establishment of a hospital for the reception of foundlings. In a similar vein to Coram's petition, the writing oscillates between two registers. On the one hand, Bray appeals to mercy for innocent children who he claims can be turned "useful"; on the other, he vividly describes the children as revolting outgrowths disfiguring the body of the nation. He puts it as follows: "by being withal put out to Service and honest Occupations, they would be moreover rendered useful Members of the Commonwealth, and not left to remain like Warts and Wens, and other filthy Excrescencies, to the defacing and weakening of the Body Politick."[46]

In 1737 Coram drafted a separate petition to be signed by men from the gentry, commercial classes, nobility, and judiciary that—like the other documents mentioned—again places claims of compassion and concern next to renditions inspiring disgust. Beyond mere survival—which by itself seems not have been considered a convincing enough motif in any of the sources—the saved children would be rendered "useful to the Publick" by the assured support of rich persons:

[45] Thomas Coram, 'Petition to the King George II', 1729, as quoted in *An Account of the Methods for the Establishment of an Hospital*, 1749 (TLA: A/FH/A/01/005/001, from Coram's Foundling Hospital Archives), p. iv.

[46] Thomas Bray, *Memorial concerning the Erecting in the City of London or the Suburbs thereof an Orphanotrophy or Hospital for the Reception of Poor Cast-off Children or Foundlings* (London: 1728), p. 16.

Most humbley Sheweth
That many Ladys of Quality and Distinction being deeply
touched with Concern for the frequent Murders committed on
poor Miserable Infant Children at their Birth by their Cruel
Parents to hide their Shame and for the Inhumane Custom
of exposing Newborn Children to Perish in the Streets or the
putting out of such unhappy Foundlings to wicked and barbar-
ous Nurses who undertaking to bring them up for a small and
trifling Sum of Money do often suffer them to Starve for want
of due Sustenance and Care Or if permitted to live either turn
them into the Streets to begg or steal or Hire them out to Vicious
persons by whom they are trained up in that infamous way
of living Whereby Thefts Robberys and Murders do grievously
abound, and some of those Miserable Infants are Blinded or
Maimed or Distorted in their Limbs in order to move Pity &
Compassion and thereby become the fitter Instruments of gain
to those Vile, Mercyless Wretches.
[...]
That many [...] Persons of Distinction Sensible of the great
Necessity there now is for such an Hospital Have by another
Written Instrument set forth That a Foundation of this kind
Established under good Management would not only save the
lives of Many of your Majesties Subjects but be a Meanes of
rendering them useful to the Publick either in the Sea or Land
Service And that a Designe so humane and Charitable as
rescuing helpless Infants from inevitable Destruction cannot
fail of being Encouraged by many Rich well disposed persons
[...].[47]

Thomas Coram, 'The Memorial & Petition of Thomas Coram Gent. in behalf of great numbers of Helpless Infants daily exposed to Destruction', 1737, as quoted in Herbert Fuller Bright Compston, *Thomas Coram, Churchman, Empire Builder, and Philanthropist* (London: Society for Promoting Christian Knowledge, 1918), pp. 89–91.

At high pace and nearly without punctuation, Coram
recounts with agitation the many fates of the "Miserable
Infants", and gets carried away in detailed descriptions of
infanticide and abuse: They are either directly killed by
their parents, exposed to "Perish in the Streets", starved
by "wicked and barbarous Nurses", or "if permitted to
live", they are hired out, made to beg and steal, or are
"Blinded or Maimed or Distorted in their limbs" with
the objective of eliciting donations. These descriptions
are intended to shock, and, in a second step, to arouse
the monarch's sympathy. Contempt is expressed for the
fact that abandoned children are used "to move Pity &
Compassion" for the gain of "Vile, Mercyless Wretches".
At the same time, the petition advocates that the children
should be employed "either in the Sea or Land Service".
As sailors or soldiers, they would be of use to the British
Empire—a self-evidently desirable end. The reason for

the outcry is therefore not *that* the "poor Miserable Infant Children" are being used for the benefit of others, but for *whose* benefit. The children's presentation "to move Pity & Compassion" in others will become important as Coram's philanthropic project advances.

THE BIRTH OF THE CONTEMPORARY ART INSTITUTION IN A CARE FACILITY FOR "DESERTED YOUNG CHILDREN"

Coram's initiative received a Royal Charter in 1739, incorporating the Hospital for the Maintenance and Education of Exposed and Deserted Young Children under a board of Governors approved by King George II.[48] From the 172 Governors initially appointed—all men chosen for their wealth and influence—fifty were elected onto the General Committee that steered the institution. Two years after its incorporation, the first children were brought by their mothers to a temporary location of what was subsequently known as the Foundling Hospital. A mother had the right to reclaim her child. Therefore, upon admission, it was assigned a serial number. In addition, personal objects were kept as tokens, that served as unique identifiers. These tokens were sealed in entry billets as a form of provenance.[49] However, it was rare for a child to be reclaimed, as one of the main motives for abandoning children was to alleviate poverty, and drastic changes in a poor mother's economic situation were unlikely.[50]

The financing of its services was a core concern to the Foundling Hospital. The royal support did not change the circumstance that the institution depended mainly on private donations to build its permanent home and to cover its costs. Hence, the most pressing issues were how to attract influential people to the Hospital in order to convince the public of the institution's respectable nature, and how to gain the financial support of rich people by appealing to their compassion.

In London, beggars' self-representation strategies usually involved the highlighting of their disabilities and wounds to elicit donations from the rich. "Filth, a lack of linen, rags [...] provided visual cues that allowed [...] elite men and women to reassure themselves about the real need and desperation of the recipients of their casual charity."[51] If the Hospital wanted to stand out, and even persuade an elite to visit it at its out-of-town

[48] Foundling Hospital (London, England), *Copy of the Royal Charter Establishing an Hospital for the Maintenance and Education of Exposed and Deserted Young Children* (London: Printed for J. Osborn, at the Golden-Ball in Paternoster Row, 1739).

[49] Maria Zytaruk, 'Artifacts of Elegy: The Foundling Hospital Tokens', *Journal of British Studies* 54, no. 2 (2015), pp. 320–22.

[50] See Alysa Levene, *Childcare, Health and Mortality in the London Foundling Hospital, 1741–1800: 'Left to the mercy of the world'* (Manchester: Manchester University Press, 2007), p. 36.

[51] Tim Hitchcock, *Down and Out in Eighteenth-Century London* (London: Hambledon and London, 2004), p. 107.

location, it had to come up with a different strategy. Rather than emphasising the foundlings' misery for the visitors, it was decided to present their situation in an idealised and agreeable way. The children were shown not in rags, but clean and in uniforms. The focus was on demonstrating the positive impact of philanthropy, and not on the destitute state of the foundlings, half of whom died, in fact, even in successful times [FIG. 4].

But would the staged presentation of foundlings suffice? What else was needed to secure a visit from potential donors? The answer was contemporary art. Abandoned children and contemporary art, in an intriguing and novel combination, were what attracted wealthy people. A Picture Gallery was built into the Hospital, in which works of art by the most respected British artists of the time were exhibited. In addition, there was a Court Room, embellished with a Rococo ceiling and yet more paintings. This turned a care facility for deserted children into Britain's first gallery for contemporary art. In the Court Room, which also served as a venue for the meetings of the Governors of the Foundling Hospital, four large paintings depicting biblical scenes were on display, showing compassionate gestures to exemplify the institution's virtuous mission. The Hospital was located in open fields, and in the 1740s and '50s, was the only place showcasing art to a—wealthy and mobile—public in Britain. The paintings as well as the neat foundlings were a big attraction that "drew a daily crowd of spectators in their splendid equipages; and a visit to the Foundling became the most fashionable morning lounge in the Reign of George II."[52] The exhibitions provided a space where donors could mingle with other members of their class and identify with the representations of charity. Two of the paintings in the Court Room, by leading painters Francis Hayman and William Hogarth [FIG. 5 AND 6], depicted the archetypal foundling Moses, once as a helpless infant saved from the river banks of the Nile and brought to the Pharaoh's daughter, and once as a well-clothed child who is returned to the Pharaoh's daughter by the wet nurse who fostered him. Incidentally, the weeping wet nurse is Moses' biological mother, who had initially saved him from persecution by placing him in a basket on the river. Eight smaller roundels in the same room depicted other private London hospitals that had been established around the same time, placing

52
John Brownlow, *The History and Objects of the Foundling Hospital: With a Memoir of the Founder* (London: Printed by C. Jaques, 1865 third edition), p. 63.

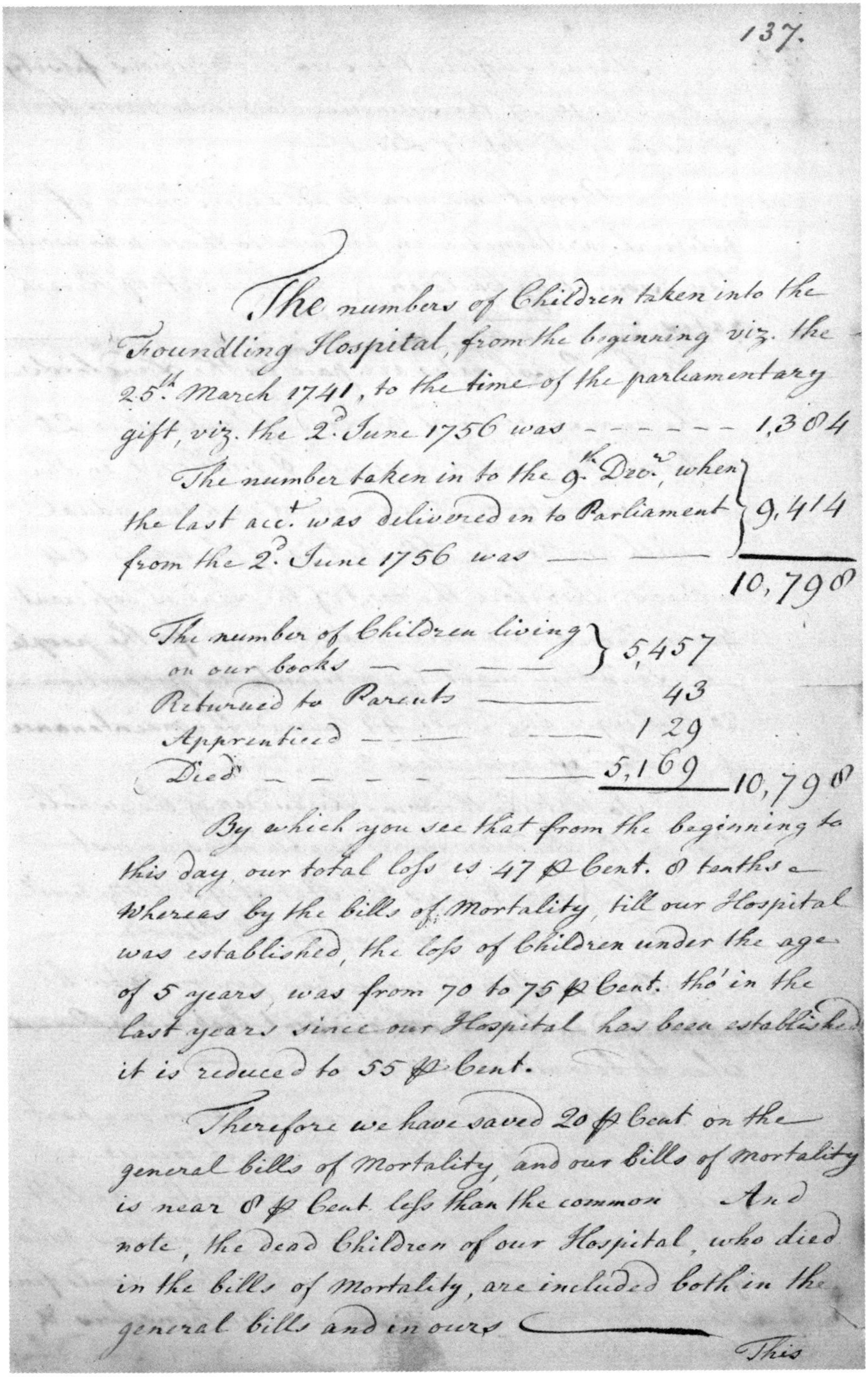

The numbers of Children taken into the Foundling Hospital, from the beginning viz. the 25th March 1741, to the time of the parliamentary gift, viz. the 2d June 1756 was — — — — — 1,384

The number taken in to the 9th Decr when the last acct was delivered in to Parliament from the 2d June 1756 was — — } 9,414
______
10,798

The number of Children living on our books — — — — } 5,457
Returned to Parents — — — — 43
Apprenticed — — — — — 129
Died — — — — — — 5,169 — 10,798

By which you see that from the beginning to this day, our total loss is 47 ℔ Cent. & tenths — Whereas by the bills of Mortality, till our Hospital was established, the loss of Children under the age of 5 years, was from 70 to 75 ℔ Cent. tho' in the last years since our Hospital has been established it is reduced to 55 ℔ Cent.

Therefore we have saved 20 ℔ Cent. on the general bills of Mortality, and our bills of Mortality is near 8 ℔ Cent. less than the common — And note, the dead Children of our Hospital, who died in the bills of Mortality, are included both in the general bills and in ours — — —

This

FIG. 4
'The number of Children taken into the Foundling Hospital, from 1741–1756',
in *Manuscript copies including Coram's petition to King…* (The London Archives,
A/FH/A/01/004, from Coram's Foundling Hospital Archives), p. 137. Ⓒ Coram

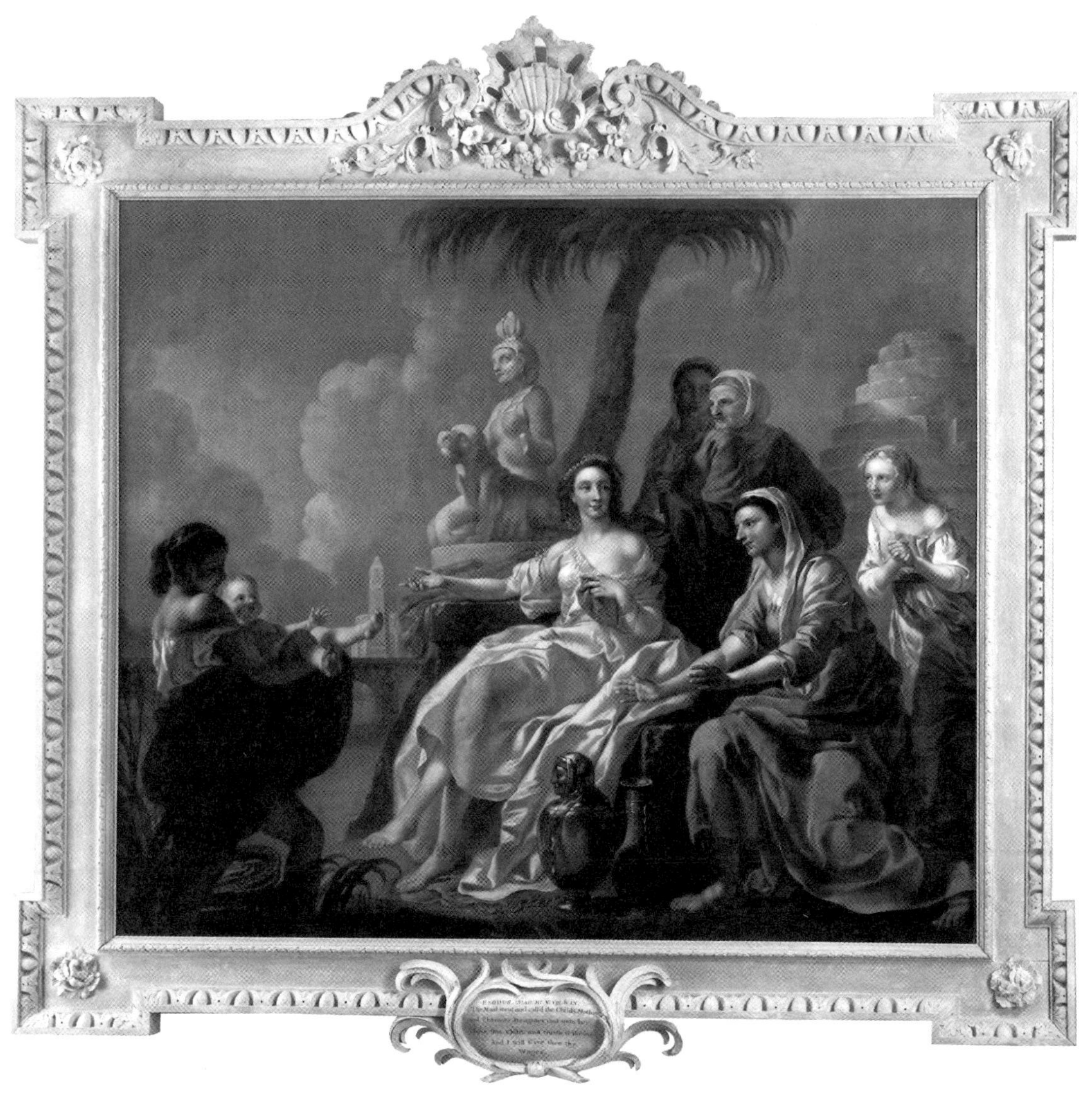

FIG. 5
Francis Hayman, *The Finding of Infant Moses in the Bullrushes*, 1746. Oil on canvas, 170.8 × 188.6 cm.
Coram in the care of the Foundling Museum

FIG. 6
William Hogarth, *Moses Brought Before Pharaoh's Daughter*, 1746. Oil on canvas, 172.7 × 208.3 cm.
Coram in the care of the Foundling Museum

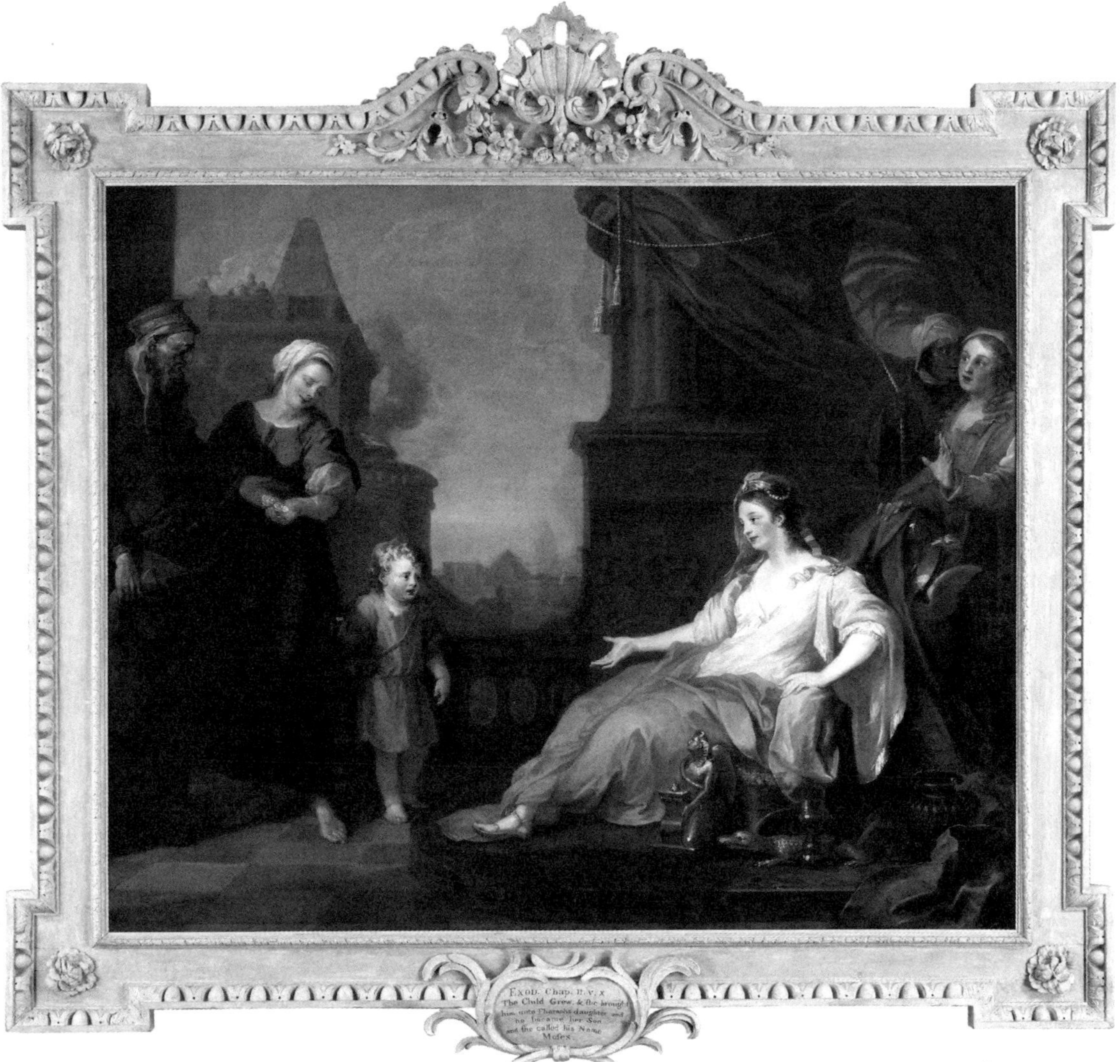

the Foundling Hospital in a chorus of private initiatives that claimed to positively shape the nation.

The Hospital was built to accommodate two different levels of clientele, who were to experience it in very different ways. These two groups coexisted without a true contact zone, their respective positions being clearly defined and separated. The building represented an imposing facility of care and education to the poor, where desperate mothers could dispose of their children if they could not provide for them. At the same time, the institution acted as a site of polite and rational assembly for its wealthy supporters, who were meant to feel at home. These dichotomous meanings are expressed in two engravings after designs by Samuel Wale, both titled *A Perspective View of the Foundling Hospital, with Emblematic Figures* [FIG. 7 AND 8]. The main entrance to the Hospital is depicted from two different angles, emphasising the contrasting messages the institution's structure was intended to convey to impoverished mothers on the one hand and affluent visitors on the other.

The presentation of the foundlings in the same building as contemporary art created a setting in which the spectators of art could compare depictions of charity with a staged reality, and thus inscribe themselves into biblical themes. Misery must be understood as diffracted and transfigured both in the paintings and in actuality. The visitors' compassionate gazes travel back and forth between an abandoned child existing there in front of them and, for instance, Moses in a painting. The resulting superposition of two different objects reinforces and reassures the patrons of their social virtue, and allows them to clearly identify their own position. What cultural theorist Lauren Berlant phrases, in a different context and time, is relevant when read against the backdrop of the Foundling Hospital and its wealthy patrons and Governors, who met there to view art but also the objects of their charity. Berlant suggests "that when suffering is presented to you in a way that invites the gift of your compassion, compassion can feel like the apex of affective agency among strangers."[53] This "apex of affective agency among strangers" resonates with the new social habits and practices of the commercial classes, in which shared feelings were central to producing a sense of belonging and joint investment.

53 Lauren Berlant, 'Introduction: Compassion (and Withholding)', in *Compassion: The Culture and Politics of an Emotion*, edited by Lauren Berlant (New York: Routledge, 2004), p. 9.

At this point, it is necessary to further situate the role of compassion as a moral sentiment in its time in order to understand the commercial classes' investment in the Foundling Hospital in greater nuance. In a period of immense visible misery and suffering, a circumstance that troubled many in regard to their Christian faith and moral obligations, a series of contemporary sources reflect a new emphasis on sentiments with respect to public life. As becomes clear, philosophical conceptions of art and morality helped to define specific public emotions as desirable within a reality of unequal social relations. At the same time as rationality became a central virtue within polite culture, moral sentiments would testify to a person's righteousness and integrity of character. Rationality and feeling, as much as self-interest and public-mindedness, were no longer regarded as mutually exclusive, but—in the right setup—as complementary. Noble emotions would lastly distinguish the refined and rational from those expressing feelings excessively, such as the economically desperate. In that regard, compassion was the object of much consideration and became the affective basis for charity and philanthropy. Compassion emerged as a moral feeling elevating those capable of feeling it over those inspiring the emotion. Somebody else's misery came to be seen not necessarily as a circumstance to be remedied, but as an opportunity to access and feel superior moral sentiments. Displays of suffering held the potential to produce generous emotions and moral growth in the wealthy. This ultimately gave misery and suffering a social function, turning them productive. As the commercial classes furthered their political endeavours through private charities, compassion became instrumental in wedding economic self-interest to expressions of benevolence.

Turnbull brought these contemporary concerns around affect and social virtue into theoretical art discourse. In *A Treatise on Ancient Painting*, he describes "[w]hatever touches our publick Sense, or calls into Action our generous, tender, and kind Affections" as that "which most agreeably detains our Mind".[54] The term "publick sense" describes the public-mindedness of a wealthy man who, because he has created the financial conditions, is able to demonstrate care for society. His exercise of

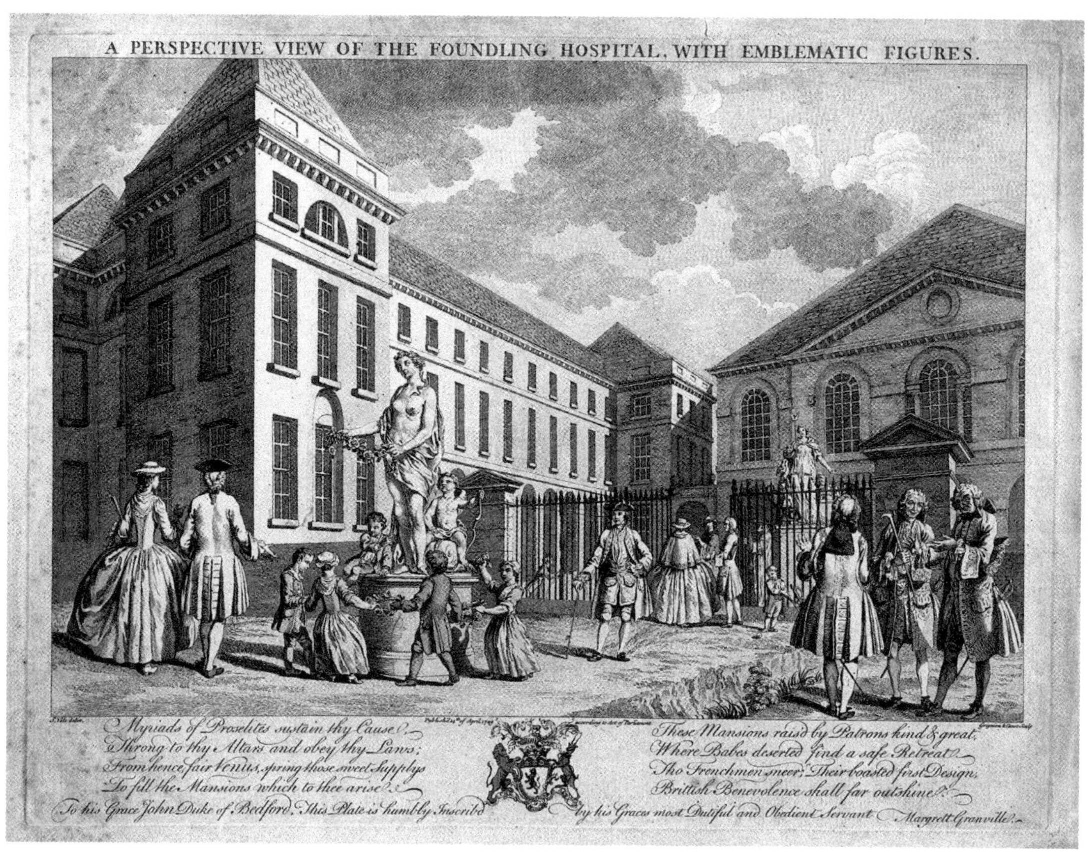

FIG. 7
Charles Grignion after Samuel Wale, *A perspective View of the Foundling Hospital, with Emblematic Figures (I)*, 1749. Engraving, 8.4 × 14.2 cm. Wellcome Collection

FIG. 8

Charles Grignion after Samuel Wale, *A perspective View of the Foundling Hospital, with Emblematic Figures (II)*, 1749. Engraving, 35.3 × 46.2 cm. Wellcome Collection

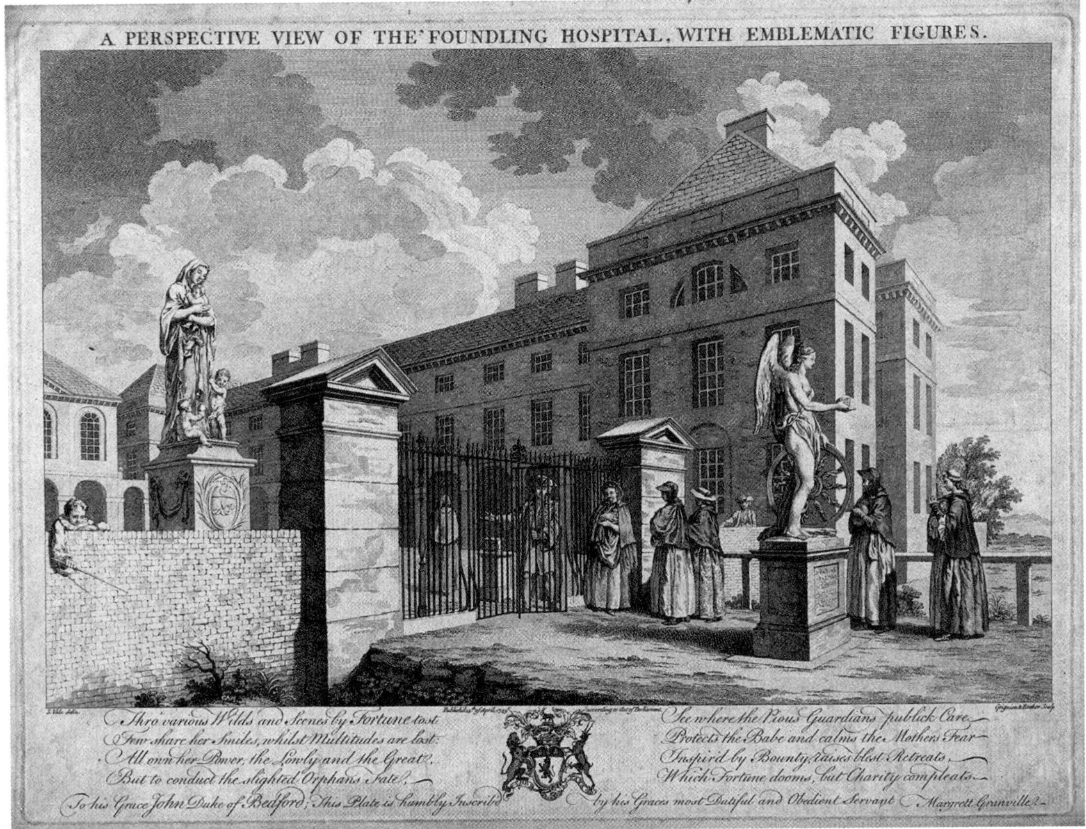

benevolence is then rewarded with positive feelings and thoughts. Turnbull ascribes to art a central function in this regard. Works of art that "call forth our Pity and Compassion into Exercise" are declared to "give us the highest Satisfaction".[55] Moral works of art, as Turnbull conceives them, are capable of instilling in the viewer a sense of goodness. Misery, it is important to note, however, in this constellation never meets the viewer raw. If compassion is inspired by art, then misery is necessarily mediated. What arouses "generous, tender, and kind Affections" is not actual misery but its representation. It is the artist who imagines for misery an aesthetic form from which "the highest Satisfaction" can be derived. Thereby, artistic renderings create an agreeable distance from which to engage with other people's suffering. Art, after all, carries the capacity for transfiguring concrete instances of social violence into vivid form, and for creating environments in which misery can be confronted with reduced inconvenience to the spectator. The misery of one group of people in this constellation, frequently rooted in social matters, becomes the topic through which artists can tease out the social feelings of another group of people. Artists' work in this regard is the production of objects which inspire compassion for the moral delight of those "qualified by Nature to receive high Pleasure from social Affections".[56]

Moral philosopher and economist Adam Smith similarly frames compassion as a sentiment morally ennobling those who are in a position to feel it. In 1759, seven years before publishing *An Inquiry into the Nature and Causes of the Wealth of Nations*,[57] in which he lays the foundations for free market economic theory, Smith published *The Theory of Moral Sentiments*, for which he received significantly more acclaim during his lifetime. In his book on moral virtue, affect in regard to spectatorship plays a crucial role, and considerations around the witnessing of misery provide important underpinnings to his later work. In *Moral Sentiments*, sympathy[58] and compassion achieve, in a moral context, what self-interest later does in an economic one: they create a supposedly natural harmony in which all parties specialise in producing what they can produce most efficiently, and relations become measured in terms of advantage. What in *The Wealth of Nations* becomes a question of trade between countries is first introduced in Smith's philosophical work as a provision of social relations.

[55]
George Turnbull, *A Treatise on Ancient Painting* (1740), p. 141.

[56]
Ibid., pp. 141–42.

[57]
Adam Smith, *An Inquiry into the Nature and Causes of the Wealth of Nations. In Two Volumes* (London: Printed for W. Strahan and T. Cadell, 1776).

[58]
The word sympathy as used in Smith's writing is closer in today's terms to the word empathy.

In *Moral Sentiments*, Smith defines "pity and compassion" as "the emotion we feel for the misery of others, when we either see it, or are made to conceive it in a very lively manner."[59] The "we" who "feel[s] for the misery of others" is clearly separated from the person suffering. These distinct positions are important throughout: The "we" becomes synonymous with a spectator who can either witness misery or be "made to conceive it in a lively manner", but is never discussed as a potential sufferer. Smith assumes a universal sympathy with misery and sorrow in human nature. However, he makes sure to distinguish the emotional excessiveness of the sufferer from the sensibility and rationality of the compassionate subject:

Though sorrow is excessive, we may still have some fellow-feeling with it. [...] We do not weep, and exclaim, and lament, with the sufferer. We are sensible, on the contrary, of his weakness and of the extravagance of his passion, and yet often feel a very sensible concern upon his account.[60]

Smith goes on to argue why an observer is naturally more drawn to another's suffering than to their pleasure. According to Smith, displays of joy evoke contempt, but the pungent sensation of pain, even when experienced only second-hand, offers a "lively and distinct perception":

The man who skips and dances about with that intemperate and senseless joy which we cannot accompany him in, is the object of our contempt and indignation. Pain besides, whether of mind or body, is a more pungent sensation than pleasure, and our sympathy with pain, though it falls greatly short of what is naturally felt by the sufferer, is generally a more lively and distinct perception than our sympathy with pleasure [...].[61]

For Smith, the contempt for the "man who skips and dances about with that intemperate and senseless joy" seems to be rooted in the circumstance that "we cannot accompany him in [it]". In the case of compassion, conversely, it is precisely the distance between observer and sufferer that ensures the agreeable nature of the feeling. If both observed states are marked as excessive, yet only one produces negative reactions, this indicates that it is not the excessiveness of emotion that is the problem. What might explain Smith's irritation with the skipping

[59] Adam Smith, *The Theory of Moral Sentiments* (London: Printed for A. Millar and A. Kincaid and J. Bell, 1759), p. 1.

[60] Ibid., p. 94.

[61] Ibid., pp. 94–95.

man, so vividly described, is his principle of advantage, as later applied to economic relations. In terms of affective experience, the skipping man has an advantage over Smith's spectator. In the scenario of pain and suffering, by contrast, the positions of advantage and disadvantage are reversed. Compassion naturally assumes a social relation in which the person regarding the suffering is in an advantageous position relative to the person experiencing it first-hand. From the perspective of the spectator, the sufferer must not leave the position of suffering, so as to keep inspiring empathic emotions. What further complicates this relation is Smith's instruction on how the spectator is to generate compassion:

The compassion of the spectator must arise altogether from the consideration of what he himself would feel if he was reduced to the same unhappy situation, and, what perhaps is impossible, was at the same time able to regard it with his present reason and judgment.[62]

It is clear that Smith's spectator can only access compassion precisely because he is not in the "unhappy situation" of suffering. Nevertheless, he is instructed to project himself into the affected position of the sufferer while simultaneously remaining in his own, removed position as a spectator. This describes a paradoxical scene in which the compassionate subject must both imagine how it would feel to suffer and view the situation from the position of sympathetic unaffectedness, which is presented as a prerequisite for reason. From a contemplative distance, actual suffering serves to stir the spectator's imagination—without, however, disagreeably affecting his sense of being in control. In this conception, the compassionate subject is naturally elevated above the poor sufferer, who serves primarily as an inspiration. Reason and judgment—available exclusively to the spectator within Smith's distinctly separate positions—then almost appear as safeguards against ending up in the position of the sufferer in the first place.

[62] Adam Smith, *The Theory of Moral Sentiments* (London: Printed for A. Millar and A. Kincaid and J. Bell, 1759), p. 10.

[63] Hogarth was born in London to a lower-middle class family that underwent periods of mixed fortune. His father's unsuccessful business endeavour—he took the leap to open London's only Latin-speaking coffee house—left the family bankrupt. A newspaper advertisement from Hogarth's Coffee House in St. John Gate from January 1704 can be found in this resourceful reference book of coffee houses of the 17th, 18th and 19th centuries: Bryant Lillywhite, *London Coffee Houses* (1963), pp. 269–70.

At the Foundling Hospital, the distinct positions of the patrons and the children were clearly defined. There was no doubt as to who was the benefactor and who was the recipient of charity, who was the viewing subject and who was the observed object. The artists involved in the project helped to give shape to these opposite positions, hoping that their contributions would lead to opportunities that they could use to their advantage. William Hogarth,[63] who, as an artist, was highly established at the time, was one of the founding Governors of the Hospital. He designed the Hospital's Coat of Arms [FIG. 9], as well as the children's uniforms, which were integral to their presentation to the visitors. Apart from donating his own works, he also convinced many other of the most prominent British artists of his time—such as Joseph Highmore, Joshua Reynolds, James Wills, Richard Wilson, Francis Hayman, Samuel Wale, Thomas Gainsborough— to follow suit. The artists were keen to connect with circles that would help them achieve greater professional success. Apart from their contributions to a charitable organisation gaining them prestige, the institutional display of their works was a novel opportunity the artists hoped to capitalise on. Since places for artists to publicly exhibit did not yet exist at that time, exposure for their work was a valuable prospect. They could bring their art to the attention of the institution's wealthy visitors, and make contact with some of the influential Governors of the Hospital. In giving select works to the Hospital, the artists wished to attract patronage, and secure future commissions or purchases. The artists also agreed to producing portraits of the Hospital's important donors, which were hung in the foundling's dining room, reminding the children to whom they owed their gratitude.[64] In return for this generosity towards the institution, the artists were awarded the title of Artist Governors, an important social recognition at a time when no other professional distinctions for artists existed. As Artist Governors, they enjoyed the right to hold annual dinners in the Hospital's Court Room, a privilege they used to cultivate contacts and hatch plans.[65]

IMPERIAL INTERESTS AND COLONIAL INHERITANCES

The influential Governors of the Foundling Hospital, whose attention the Artist Governors desired, were members of the commercial classes. Their stakes in charity reflected their ascension to wealth. Visible manifestations of their social virtues were intended to substantiate their

[64] A circumstance that is commonly overlooked is that this made the foundlings some of the earliest spectators of contemporary art in Britain. No records exist, however, regarding their reactions to these paintings.

[65] The artists were not the only people offering their work without compensation. The construction of the Hospital building relied heavily on the involvement of middle-class professionals and businessmen, such as amateur architect Theodore Jacobson, and surveyor James Horne, who also provided their services for free. In most cases, their commitment to the project proved beneficial for them, as the contacts they made through it were helpful in securing future employment. See Alan Borg, 'Theodore Jacobsen and the building of the Foundling Hospital', *The Georgian Group Journal*, vol. 13 (2003), pp. 12–34; Steven Parissien, 'The architecture of the Foundling Hospital', in *Enlightened Self-Interest: The Foundling Hospital and Hogarth*, edited by Rhian Harris and Robin Simon (London: Draig Press, 1997), p. 26.

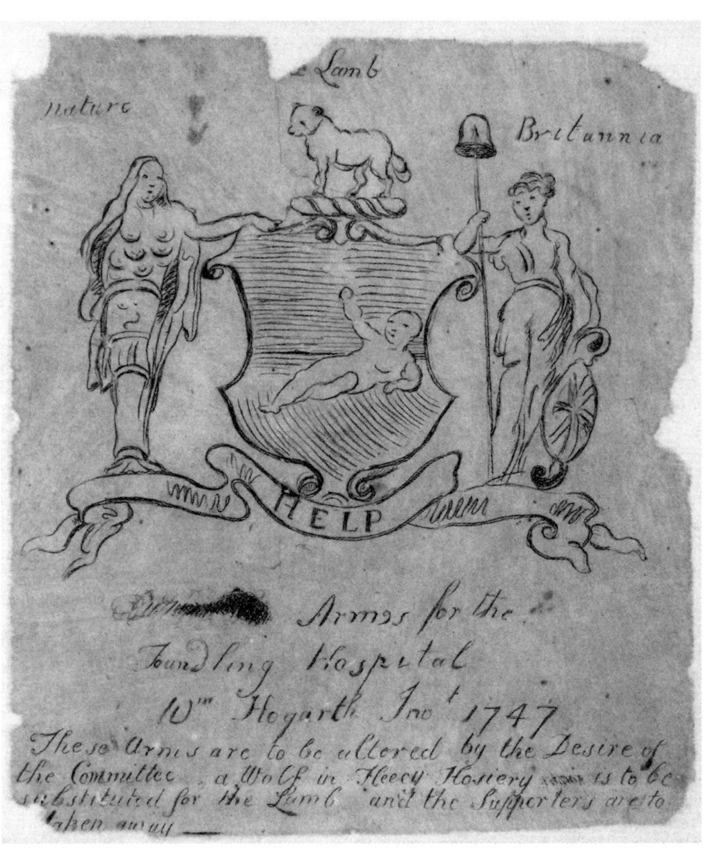

FIG. 9
William Hogarth, *Arms for the Foundling Hospital*, 1747. Drawing,
15.3 × 13 cm. Coram in the care of the Foundling Museum

claims to leading positions within British citizenry and serve as evidence of their public-mindedness. Many on the list of Governors were traders, merchants and industrialists from London whose businesses relied on imports from the colonies. In addition, a significant number of Governors lived overseas.[66] These were plantation owners, colonists and slavers, amongst whom were the institution's most important financial contributors. The donor portraits painted by the artists therefore feature some of the time's most prominent colonial barons.

The Hospital's objectives were closely aligned with the commercial and political interests of its Governors and supporters. The first *Regulations for Managing the Hospital for Exposed and Deserted Young Children*, from 1742, assign the children different roles within the system of the triangular trade. In line with what Coram had originally envisaged in his petitions, the foundlings were to be "made useful":

It is hoped that for the easier disposal of the Boys an order may be obtained from the Lords of the Admiralty to the Captains of his Majesty's Ships to take a certain Number of Boys from time to time [...], and if the Captain of every Merchant Ship [...] was obliged if required to take one or more it would greatly increase the Number of Seamen [...].
[T]he Girls are to be placed out, as Household Servants, or put out for a Term of Years to be employed in the Linnen or Woolen Manufactory as soon as possible [...].[67]

The procedures and objectives defined in the earliest regulations were duly put into practice, as a correspondence from 1759 confirms. In a letter, the treasurer of the Hospital outlines the typical protocol for the upbringing of male foundlings:

Whatever Subject is Saved, and reared by this Institution, will, in process of time, add to the greatness and natural strength of the Kingdom. [...] The Children are nursed in the Country, and when able are taught to Labour in the open Air, when it can be done. They are early placed out Apprentice, some at 9 or 10 Years old, and many sent to the Sea in Severe Climates, have been found healthy, and useful.[68]

The children who were "sent to the Sea" at an early age became useful to the British Empire, but also to individuals profiting from the triangular trade. This circumstance

[66] For a full list of founding Governors see Foundling Hospital (London, England), *A List of the Present Governors and Guardians of the Hospital for the Maintenance and Education of Exposed and Deserted Young Children, Incorporated by His Majesty's Royal Charter, Bearing Date the 17th Day of October, 1739, and Elected since to the 25th of June, 1740* (London: 1740).

[67] 'The Methods of Placing them out to proper Employments', in *The Regulations for Managing the Hospital for Exposed and Deserted Young Children, 1742* (TLA: A/FH/A/06/015/001, from Coram's Foundling Hospital Archives).

[68] 'Letter from Hospital Treasurer Mr Taylor White to Mr Potter, February 1759', in *Manuscript copies including Coram's petition to King...* (TLA: A/FH/A/01/004, from Coram's Foundling Hospital Archives), pp. 148, 152.

secured the Foundling Hospital support from its Governors and supporters in the colonies, whose operations were protected by "the greatness and natural strength of the Kingdom". From these supporters the Hospital inherited plantations and estates, which it either sold or leased.

Henry Needham, for instance, a wealthy Irish assemblyman, landowner and slaver in Jamaica, was one of the Hospital's biggest donors. In his will, he stipulated that the Hospital should inherit plantations of his in Jamaica.[69] His brother Robert, however, wanted to remain in possession of the estate and disputed that Henry had the power to pass it on to the Hospital. To avoid controversies, Robert made an agreement with the Governors of the Hospital. In order to maintain the plantations under his care, he paid more than 5,000 pounds in compensation,[70] a sum sufficient to cover the Hospital's expenses for an entire year.[71]

William Williams, also a plantation owner and slaver in Jamaica, was another important funder of the Hospital. He too mentioned estates in Jamaica in his will that were to be sold for the benefit of the Foundling Hospital. Expressly included in the inheritance are enslaved persons and their descendants. The will from 1759 stipulates:

[...] *to sell the same* [property in Jamaica], *together with all and every the Negro, Mulatto, and other slaves whatsoever to me belonging, with their future offspring, issue, or increase, and pay the net proceeds to the Treasurer of the Foundling Hospital.*[72]

In 1766, the Hospital leased the same estates to four of its Governors: Taylor White, jurist, art collector, and long-time treasurer of the Foundling Hospital; Gilbert Ford of St Catherine, attorney-general to Jamaica; John Cruikshank, provost-marshal of Jamaica; and Charles Child, merchant and insurance broker involved in the East India Company [FIG. 10]. The wording of the lease agreement is in many places almost identical to that of Williams' will.[73] This legacy also brought the Hospital over 5,000 pounds in income.[74]

A comparison of the hospital's annual expenditure with the sums derived from these colonial legacies proves that the education and care of abandoned children in London was directly based on the sale and labour of enslaved people on the supposed margins of the British Empire. Identifying these linkages is important not only

[69] A hand-written case description of the bequest of Henry Needham is part of a bundle of miscellaneous documents. See *Legal Proceedings in Chancery, 1758–59* (TLA: A/FH/A/22/002/017 from Coram's Foundling Hospital Archives).

[70] See *An Act for Carrying into Execution an Agreement between the Governors [...] and Robert Nedham [...] relating to an Estate in the Island of Jamaica, 1762* (TLA: A/FH/M/01/004/004, from Coram's Foundling Hospital Archives), p. 1.

[71] The necessary annual expenses, exclusive of the buildings, are stated to amount "to upwards of 5000l". See 'Account of the Foundling Hospital', in *The London Magazine* (London: 1757), p. 88.

[72] The will of William Williams from 1759 as quoted in John Brownlow, *The History and Objects of the Foundling Hospital* (1865), p. 51.

[73] See *Assignment of Equitable Interest & Lease of Plantations in Jamaica, 1766* (TLA: A/FH/A/16/013/030, from Coram's Foundling Hospital Archives).

[74] "The legacy yielded to the charity £5563." John Brownlow, *The History and Objects of the Foundling Hospital* (1865), p. 52.

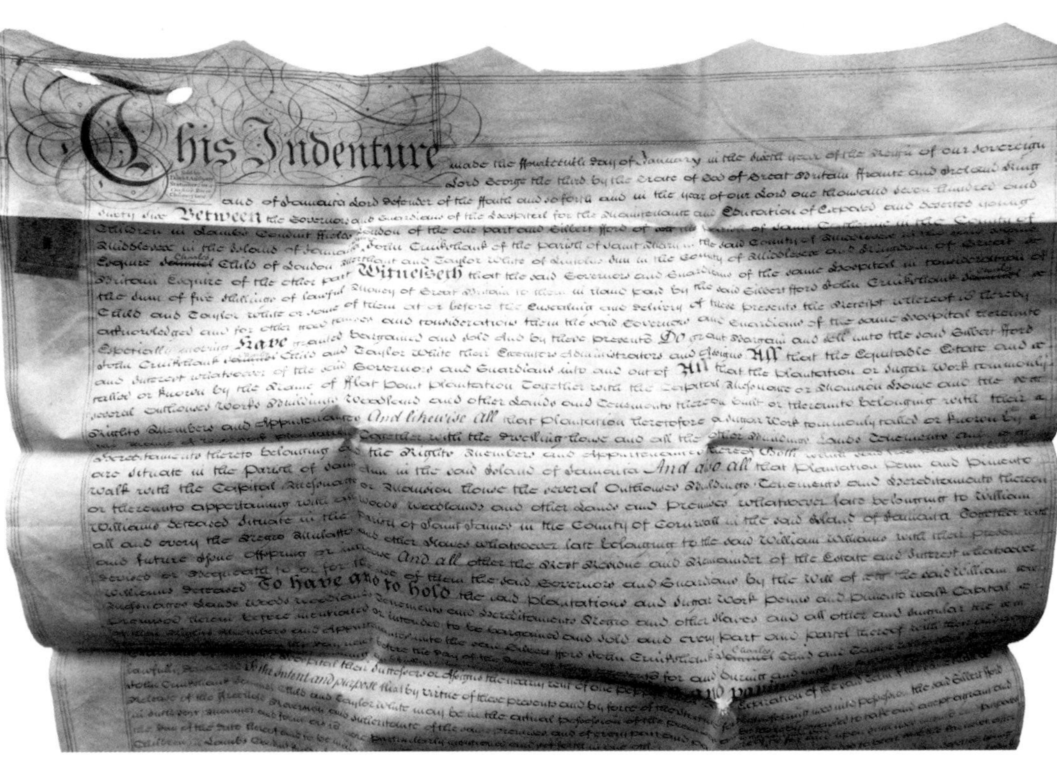

FIG. 10

Assignment of Equitable Interest & Lease of Plantations in Jamaica, 1766 (The London Archives, A/FH/A/16/013/030, from Coram's Foundling Hospital Archives). © Coram

in relation to the Foundling Hospital as a care facility, but also as an art institution. The microcosm of the Hospital was connected to a larger whole, which is also how contemporary art intertwines with these realities. If this specific historical context is understood as a genesis of the contemporary art institution, this genesis must be recognised as materially rooted in colonial violence. A cycle can be recognised in which contemporary art attracts donors to an institution; the donors' contributions keep the institution running and help keep abandoned children alive in London; these children are brought up to serve the expansion of the British Empire as well as businessmen with colonial interests; the colonialists in turn finance the institution in which contemporary art is exhibited.

Artists actively shaped the Foundling Hospital, and hoped to capitalise on the opportunities offered by proximity to wealth and power. As it turns out, subsequent developments initiated by the same group of artists would solidify these relations, and anchor the institutionalisation of contemporary art even more firmly in them.

[75] Thomas Mortimer (compiler), *A Concise Account of the Rise, Progress, and Present State of the Society for the Encouragement of Arts, Manufactures, and Commerce, Instituted at London, Anno MDCCLIV. Compiled from Original Papers of the first Promoters of the plan; and from other authentic records* (London: 1763), p. 12.

THE INVENTION OF THE ENTRANCE FEE, OR: CONTEMPORARY ART MEETS A PUBLIC IT DOESN'T WANT

In 1754, English painter William Shipley founded the Society for Encouragement of Arts, Manufactures and Commerce, as he put it, "to embolden enterprize, to enlarge Science, to refine Art, to improve our Manufactures and extend our Commerce, in a word, to render Great Britain the School of instruction, as it is already the centre of traffic to the greatest part of the known world."[75] The Society of Arts—as it is commonly shortened to—was a private organisation that consisted mainly of merchants and other members of the commercial classes who, through it, pursued their own interests. They considered innovation necessary for the advancement of manufacturing and agriculture. In order to spark these innovations, art education was identified as crucial for the development of skills that were useful for both domestic industrialisation and colonial projects: maps had to be drawn, machines had to be developed, ornaments had to be designed, etc.

To provide incentives for productivity and efficiency, the society's membership financed prizes or "premiums" as they were called. These premiums covered a vast range of affairs and transparently reflected the members' various commercial and political interests. For example, premiums were offered for the production of gunpowder in England and cotton in the American colonies, for "causing to be knit" in workhouses the largest quantity of worsted hose for women, and also for the best painting depicting English history.[76]

At one of their annual dinners, which took place in November 1759, the Artist Governors involved in the Foundling Hospital came up with the idea of organising yearly exhibitions of contemporary art. At a follow-up meeting called at short-notice in a tavern—gathering all the most established artists of that time—they decided to approach the Society of Arts about the use of their premises in the centre of London. The artists desired to exhibit their art more widely and more publicly than the Hospital's remote setting allowed, so as to broaden their fame and "justly raise them to Distinction".[77] As a result of that meeting, in early 1760 the Society of Arts received a letter from the artists, in which they formally requested the use of the Society's spaces. In the letter, the artists recognised and complimented the imperial activities of the Society's membership by stating that "the Arts will gain Dignity from the Protection of those whom the World has already learned to respect."[78] The artists presented their plan for an exhibition as a charitable initiative, in which a one shilling entry fee was "destin'd to the Support of those Artists whose Age, Infirmities or other lawful Hindrances suffer them to be no longer Candidates for Praise."[79] The Society accepted the artists' request but didn't permit them to charge an entrance fee. A compromise was reached which allowed the artists to optionally sell catalogues for sixpence.[80]

At the time, there seemed to be no doubt that a first public exhibition of contemporary art would be a great novelty, and that the broad public would indeed be excited to visit such an exhibition. Despite the Society insisting on the exhibition being free and accessible to the public, however, it preemptively drafted some measures for exclusion, mostly explicitly along the lines of class and gender. A special subcommittee appointed by the Society resolved [FIG. 11]:

That a Discretionary Power be lodged in the Officers of the Society, or whom they shall authorize, to exclude all persons whom they

[76] Minutes of the General Committee on 5 April 1758, in *The Minutes of the Society for the Encouragement of Arts, Manufactures and Commerce,* vol. III, 1758–59 (Royal Society of Arts Archives, RSA/AD/MA/100/12/01/03), pp. 22–44.

[77] Minutes from the Meeting on 12 November 1759, in *The Minutes of the General Meetings of the Artists and the Committee for managing the Public Exhibition,* 1759–63 (Royal Academy of Arts Archives, SA/1).

[78] Minutes from the Meeting on 26 February 1759, in *The Minutes of the General Meetings of the Artists, 1759–63.*

[79] Ibid.

[80] Minutes of the General Committee on 2 April 1760, in *The Minutes of the Society for the Encouragement of Arts, Manufactures and Commerce,* vol. V, 1760 (Royal Society of Arts Archives, RSA/AD/MA/100/12/01/05), p. 3.

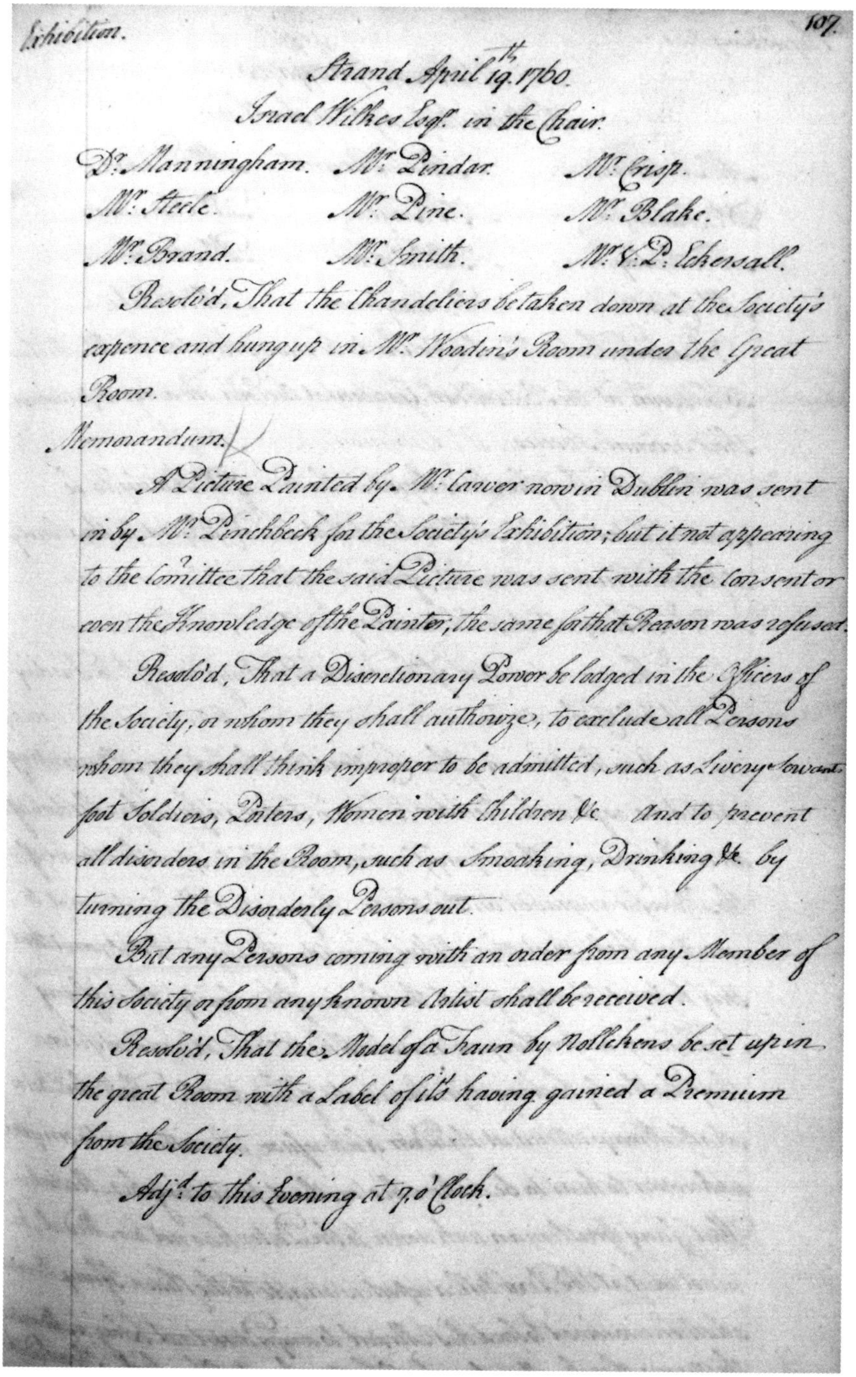

Strand April 19.th 1760.

Israel Wilkes Esq.r in the Chair.

D.r Manningham.   M.r Pindar.   M.r Crisp.
M.r Steele.   M.r Pine.   M.r Blake.
M.r Brand.   M.r Smith.   M.r & D.r Tichenall.

Resolv'd, That the Chandeliers be taken down at the Society's expence and hung up in M.r Wooden's Room under the Great Room.

Memorandum.

A Picture Painted by M.r Lawer now in Dublin was sent in by M.r Pinchbeck for the Society's Exhibition; but it not appearing to the Comittee that the said Picture was sent with the Consent or even the Knowledge of the Painter, the same for that Reason was refused.

Resolv'd, That a Discretionary Power be lodged in the Officers of the Society, or whom they shall authorize, to exclude all Persons whom they shall think improper to be admitted, such as Livery Servants, foot Soldiers, Porters, Women with Children &c. And to prevent all disorders in the Room, such as Smoaking, Drinking &c. by turning the Disorderly Persons out.

But any Persons coming with an order from any Member of this Society or from any known Artist shall be received.

Resolv'd, That the Model of a Faun by Nollekens be set up in the great Room with a Label of its having gained a Premium from the Society.

Adj.d to this Evening at 7. o'Clock.

FIG. 11
Minutes of the Committee for the Exhibition, 19 April 1760, in *Minutes of the Committees of the Society for the Encouragement of Arts, Manufactures and Commerce, 1758–60* (Royal Society of Arts Archives, RSA/PR/GE/112/12/1), p. 107.
© RSA Archives, London

shall think improper to be admitted, such as Livery Servants, foot Soldiers, Porters, Women with Children &.c And to prevent all disorders in the Room, such as Smoaking, Drinking, &.c by turning the Disorderly Persons out.[81]

The exhibition opened on 21 April 1760 in the Great Room of the Society of Arts, in the Strand, a space that could accommodate up to about 400 people.[82] Several hundred works of art by sixty-eight artists—exclusively men— were shown, including paintings, sculptures, models, engravings and drawings. The list of artists comprised many of those involved in the Foundling Hospital, such as Reynolds, Wale, Wilson and Hayman.[83] From a total of 6,582 catalogues that were sold, it can be deduced that far more people visited the exhibition during the two weeks that it was on view.[84] Economically, this first exhibition can also be counted as a great success for the artists. It created a revenue of 164 pounds, the profit of which was initially intended to be used for the support of elderly artists. After a number of resolutions at several meetings, however, these plans were changed. After expenses were covered, and a piece of plate was gifted to painter Francis Milner Newton for his service as secretary, about 82 pounds were invested in stocks for the advancement of an academy that was not described in further detail.[85] Since only eight years later the Royal Academy of Arts was founded by many of the same artists, it is reasonable to assume this plan was already in discussion at this earlier point as a future institutional framework. With this goal in mind, investing in stocks rather than providing financial aid to elderly colleagues was a priority for the artists. Financial matters and schemes were generally important topics at their meetings. In their quest for fame and institutionalisation, they responded quickly to political changes and were willing to take bold investment decisions. When George III became successor to King George II, the artists hoped that a young monarch, more inclined towards the arts, could be charmed into support- ing their plans to found an academy. Consequently, half of the sum they had put into stocks was taken out of the bank again,[86] since the artists felt the money was more promisingly invested in "Illumination and Firework on His Majesty's Birth Day".[87]

Despite the success of this first public exhibi- tion, the artists complained heavily and repeatedly about two major inconveniences (FIG. 12 AND 13). The first aspect

[81] Minutes of the Committee for the Exhibition, 19 April 1760, in *Minutes of the Committees of the Society for the Encouragement of Arts, Manufactures and Commerce, 1758–60* (Royal Society of Arts Archives, RSA/PR/GE/ 112/12/1), p. 107.

[82] Brian Allen, 'The Society of Arts and the first exhibition of contemporary art in 1760', *RSA Journal, vol. 139, no. 5416* (March 1991), p. 266.

[83] See *A Catalogue of the Pictures, Sculptures, Models, Drawings, Prints, etc. Of the present artists. Exhibited in the Great Room of the Society for the Encouragement of Arts, Manufactures, and Commerce, on the 21st of April, 1760* (London: 1760).

[84] Brian Allen, 'The Society of Arts and the first exhibition of contemporary art in 1760' (1991), p. 266.

[85] See Walpole Society (Great Britain) and A. J. Finberg, *The Sixth Volume of the Walpole Society* (Oxford: Printed for the Walpole Society by Frederick Hall at the University Press, 1917), pp. 119–20.

[86] See Minutes from the Meeting on 7 July 1761, in *The Minutes of the General Meetings of the Artists, 1759–63.*

[87] Walpole Society and A. J. Finberg, *The Sixth Volume of the Walpole Society* (1917), p. 125.

Turks Head 25th Novr 1760

This Evening the following chosen on the Committee met Vizt —

Messrs Hayman   Seaton   Mr Ardell
Wale   Wilson   Reynolds
Newton   Yeo   Wilton
Moser   Hone

Mr Hayman was unanimously elected Chairman & took
the Chair accordingly —

Resolved

That Application be made to the Society for the Society
for the Encouragement of Arts &c for the Use of their Room
That the Exhibition be the begining of June in order that
the Pictures offer'd for the Premiums may be removed.
The Artists having found great Inconvenience in lying under
the Imputation of loosing those Premiums for which they
were not Candidates.

Great Inconvenience having been found by Inferior
People crowding last year

Resolved   That the Catalogue be a Shilling & that no Person be
admitted without taking one, the same to serve as a Ticket.

Resolved   That the above Minutes be the Substance of the Letter
to be sent to the Society. Mr Reynolds is desired to request
Mr Johnson to continue his good Offices to the Artists

Adjourn'd till summoned by the Chairman

F. M. Newton Secy

Turks Head 8.th Decemr. 1760

At a Committee Present —

Mr Hayman in the Chair .

Messrs. Wilson   Moser   Reynolds
Rooker   Hone   Yeo
Mc Ardell   Wale
Seaton   Gwynn
Collins   Newton

The Minutes of the last Committee read & confirm'd.

Mr Chairman reported that he had received the Draught of a Letter from Mr Johnson as requested last Meeting, as follows —

Sir

The favour conferred last Year on the Artists by the Society has encouraged them to solicite the use of their Room for a second Exhibition.

This request may now be granted with less inconvenience to the Society, as the Exhibition will be deferred to June a Month in which the Meetings of the Society are more rare than in the Winter; the Artists being desirous that the Pictures drawn for the prize should be removed, lest any Man should a second time suffer the disgrace of having lost that which he never sought.

The Exhibition of last Year was crouded and incommoded by the intrusion of great Numbers whose Stations and education made them no proper Judges of Statuary or Painting, and who were made idle and tumultuous by the opportunity of a Shew.

It is now therefore intended that the Catalogues shall be sold for a shilling each, and none allowed to enter without a Catalogue which may serve as a ticket for admission.

These regulations which have been very deliberately formed

formed —

that irritated the artists was that they perceived their exhibition as "crowded and incommoded by the intrusion of great Numbers whose Stations and education made them no proper Judges of Statuary and Painting, and who were made idle and tumultuous by the opportunity of a shew."[88] Gwynn, author of *London and Westminster Improved*, who was also a participant in the exhibition, goes a step further in the devaluation of great parts of the audience in his summary of the exhibition:

[T]hat which was intended only as a polite, entertaining and rational amusement for the publick, became a scene of tumult and disorder; and to such a height was the rage of visiting the exhibition carried, that, when the members themselves had sat-isfied their own curiosity, the room was crowded [...] with menial servants and their acquaintance; this prostitution of the polite arts undoubtedly became extremely disagreeable to the profess-ors themselves, who heard alike, with indignation, their works censured or approved by kitchen-maids and stable-boys [...].[89]

Gwynn's notes show that—contrary to widespread assumption—there initially existed, in fact, a strong in-terest in contemporary art across social classes. However, an emergent artistic elite found "Great Inconvenience [...] by Inferior People crowding",[90] and was bothered when the rhetorically addressed "publick" actually showed up and expressed an opinion. The artists took offence in their work being assessed by an audience, who in their view, lacked the expertise to judge it. As a result, they degraded entire professional groups "and their acquaintance" as incapable of evaluating art. Remarkably, not only the negative judgment by visitors caused irrita-tion, but likewise their approval.

This echoes an assertion by Hume in his essay "Of the Standard of Taste" in which he denies those new to art the ability to make aesthetic judgments: "A man, who has had no opportunity of comparing the different kinds of beauty, is indeed totally unqualified to pronounce an opinion with regard to any object presented to him."[91] For many visitors this exhibition, being the first of its kind, was of course their first encounter with contempo-rary art. This is natural, since previously only members of the aristocracy or gentry—in the country houses—, and more recently members of the commercial classes —in the Foundling Hospital, or in artists' studios— had the opportunity to be exposed to contemporary art.

[88] Minutes from the Meeting on 8 December 1760, in *The Minutes of the General Meetings of the Artists, 1759–63*.

[89] John Gwynn, *London and Westminster Improved* (1766), pp. 24–25.

[90] Minutes from the Meeting on 25 November 1760, in *The Minutes of the General Meetings of the Artists, 1759–63*.

[91] David Hume, 'Of the Standard of Taste' (1757), p. 223.

Against this backdrop, the artists' reactions to large parts of their audience prove that they explicitly coveted the attention of the upper-middle class who—from the point of view of both the artists and contemporary philosophy—were considered qualified to express aesthetic opinions on the basis of their knowledge of art. These were also the circles the artists identified with and strove to belong to. Visitors from lower classes (kitchenmaids, stable boys, menial servants, etc.), in contrast, were marked as violent intruders in a polite environment.

The second aspect that the artists took as an insult was the circumstance that their works were exhibited alongside the works of amateur painters who had been awarded the Society's premiums for history or landscape painting. As Gwynn notes, "[t]he great inconvenience of this method of proceeding was soon discovered by several of the most eminent painters, whose reputations were already so eminently established as to prevent their becoming candidates for a trifling premium [...]."[92] Many visitors asked who had won the premiums, and concluded that this meant they were the best from all exhibited pictures. The established artists were greatly upset that the public thought that they had lost to hobbyists in an insignificant competition that they had not even entered. It would have been of no consequence, writes Gwynn, had "this injurious decision [been confined] to the vulgar spectators," but "unfortunately for the arts, many in a much higher sphere of life were liable to be led away by the same opinion [...]."[93]

The artists were determined not to exhibit again next to amateur painters who competed for a "trifling premium". Their aspiration was to establish a reputation of excellence, which in their understanding demanded that they only exhibit with artists of the same level. Before they approached the Society again to request their premises for a second exhibition, they recorded their "great Inconvenience in lying under the Imputation of loosing [sic] those Premiums for which they were not Candidates."[94] In the same meeting, they also firmly agreed that for their second exhibition "the Catalogue be a shilling and that no Person be admitted without taking one, the same to serve as a Ticket."[95] To put the price in perspective: an ordinary craftsperson would have been unlikely to be able to afford a catalogue for this price.[96]

The Society granted permission for the artists to organise a further exhibition at their premises, but

92
John Gwynn, *London and Westminster Improved* (1766), p. 25.

93
Ibid.

94
Minutes from the Meeting on 25 November 1760, in *The Minutes of the General Meetings of the Artists, 1759–63*.

95
Ibid.

96
The weekly wage of a 'good mechanic' in 1760 was about 17 shillings. See 'Chart Shewing at One View the Price of The Quarter of Wheat', and 'Wages of Labour by the Week, from The Year 1565 to 1821', in William Playfair, *A Letter to Our Agricultural Distress* (London: Printed for William Sams, 1821).

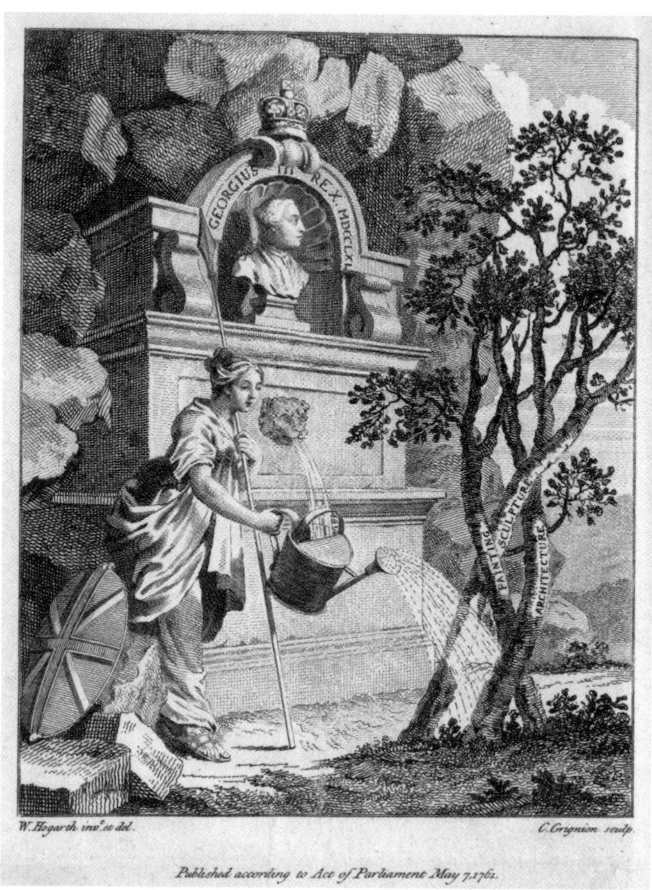

FIG. 14
Charles Grignion after William Hogarth, *Frontispiece to the Catalogue of the Pictures, Sculptures, Models, Drawings, Prints, &c. Exhibited by the Society of Artists of Great-Britain, at the Great Room in Spring-Garden*, 1761. Etching with engraving, 17.3 × 13.4 cm. © Royal Academy of Arts, London

insisted that the pictures painted for the premiums should remain, and that the exhibition had to be "free & open to the Public".[97] The artists found they couldn't comply with this, and rented another room in Spring Gardens, where their second exhibition opened in May 1761.[98] Here they were free to restrict access as they saw fit: a catalogue was sold for a shilling [FIG. 14 AND 15], and it served as a ticket for a whole family. Although producing great profit, this mode of admission was still described as "productive of crowd and disorder".[99]

This inspired the artists to adopt a more rigorous admissions policy for their exhibition the following year. For the 1762 annual exhibition, an entrance fee was charged per person, not per family. And just as is customary today, a ticket came with a free exhibition brochure: "that one Shilling be taken at the Door for Admission, every time a Catalogue given Gratis."[100] In the preface to the 1762 exhibition catalogue, the artists felt compelled to defend the newly introduced admission fee, and revealed their motives with remarkable transparency. One unambiguous conclusion they draw is that "all are desirous to see an exhibition", meaning that interest in contemporary art was present across classes. However, many of those who wanted to see the artists' exhibition the artists wanted only in theory as spectators. Instead, they marked them as misbehaving and dangerous. In the end, the artists candidly admit to desiring an affluent and cultured audience first and foremost:

Of the price put upon this Exhibition some account may be demanded. Whoever sets his work to be shown, naturally desires a multitude of spectators, but his desire defeats its own end, when spectators assemble in such numbers as to obstruct one another. Tho' we are far from wishing to diminish the pleasures, or depreciate the sentiments of any class of the community, we know however, what every one knows, that all cannot be judges or purchasers of works of art; yet we have already found by experience, that all are desirous to see an exhibition. When the terms of admission were low, our room was throng'd with such multitudes as made access dangerous, and frightened away those, whose approbation was most desired.[101]

The artists had hereby invented the admission fee for exhibitions, not with the aim of raising more money for artists—the previous exhibitions had all produced great profit—but to keep those out who they considered

[97] Minutes from the Meeting on 16 January 1761, in *The Minutes of the General Meetings of the Artists, 1759–63.*

[98] It is important to note that in contrast to the mostly more established artists who parted with the Society of Arts, another group of artists continued to exhibit annually at the Society without charging an entrance fee, and called themselves the Free Society of Artists. The group who shifted their exhibitions to Spring Gardens are usually referred to as The Society of Artists of Great Britain. See Algernon Graves, *The Society of Artists of Great Britain, 1760–1791; the Free Society of Artists, 1761–1783* (London: G. Bell and Sons, 1907).

[99] Edward Edwards, *Anecdotes of Painters, Who Have Resided or Been Born in England: With Critical Remarks on Their Productions* (London: Leigh and Sotheby, 1808), p. xxvi.

[100] Minutes from the Meeting on 13 March 1762, in *The Minutes of the General Meetings of the Artists, 1759–63.*

[101] *A Catalogue of the Pictures, Sculptures, Models, Drawings, Prints, &c. Exhibited by the Society of Artists of Great-Britain, at the Great Room in Spring Gardens, Charing-Cross, May 17th Anno 1762* (London: 1762), p. v.

incapable of judging or purchasing their work, and whose presence they felt was inappropriate. It was in the interest of the commercial classes and artists alike that the contemplative sphere of contemporary art not be confused with leisure entertainment for the masses, as it would otherwise have lost its distinctive function. The exclusion of the lower classes from the exhibition was twofold; it was both an exclusion from contemporary art and an exclusion from the emerging systems that, for the commercial classes, were an important factor in claiming social status. At the same time as knowledge about art was being established as a social currency, there was to be no misunderstanding about the relationship between art and social ascension. For advancement was not a question of culture alone, but of culture *and* money.

The structures that solidified from that moment on were built on both the artists' aspiration to gain the support of the higher strata of British citizenry, and their desire to create social spheres in which their works would be seen by those they considered their suited audience. As Gwynn describes it, the 1762 exhibition received "applause [...] by persons of the greatest taste and distinction" and showed "what a prodigious progress has been made in the arts".[102] The great success, "and the harmony which subsisted among the exhibitors, naturally led them to the thoughts of soliciting an establishment, and forming themselves into a body [...]."[103] No longer inconvenienced in their exhibitions by people they considered inferior, the artists were now ready to institute. The fireworks also paid off. In 1765 they were granted a Royal Charter from King George III, which incorporated them as The Society of Artists of Great Britain. Only three years later, many of the artists involved in the same group became founding members of the Royal Academy of the Arts, which was established as an independent, privately funded institution under royal protection.

INSTITUTING INCONVENIENCE

Contemporary art, at its earliest moment of inception, was fundamentally shaped by artists' efforts at class distinction as they strove to inscribe themselves into a new upper middle class. A group of influential artists, not the least through their self-conceptions, helped normalise and solidify specific vectors of exclusion—and with lasting

[102] John Gwynn, *London and Westminster Improved* (1766), p. 25.

[103] Ibid., pp. 25–26.

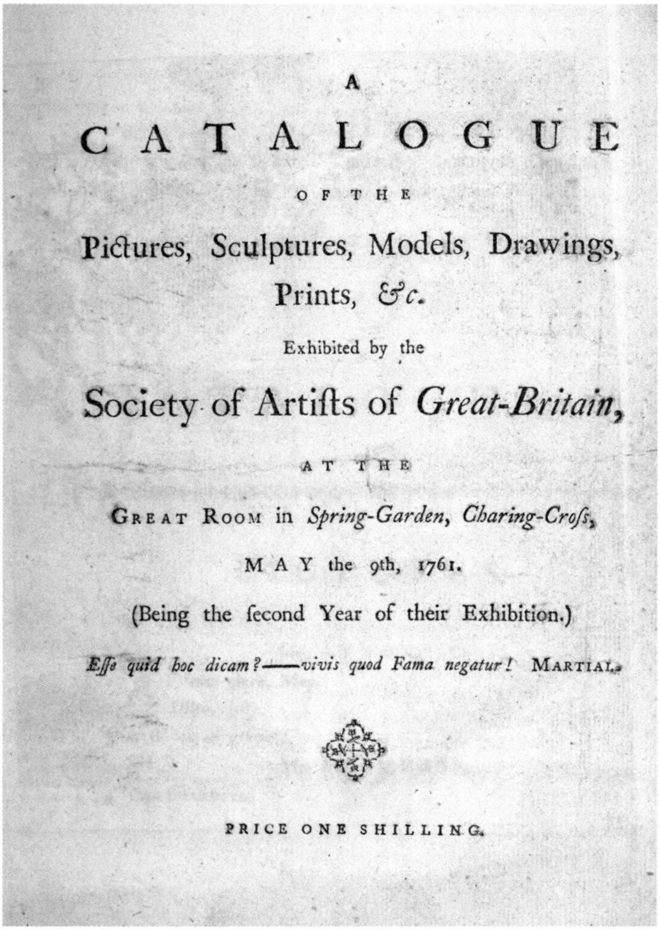

A

CATALOGUE

OF THE

Pictures, Sculptures, Models, Drawings,

Prints, &c.

Exhibited by the

Society of Artifts of *Great-Britain,*

AT THE

GREAT ROOM in *Spring-Garden, Charing-Crofs,*

MAY the 9th, 1761.

(Being the fecond Year of their Exhibition.)

Effe quid hoc dicam?——vivis quod Fama negatur! MARTIAL.

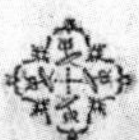

PRICE ONE SHILLING.

FIG. 15
A Catalogue of the Pictures, Sculptures, Models, Drawings,
Prints, &c. Exhibited by the Society of Artists of Great-
Britain, at the Great Room in Spring-Garden, 1761.
© Royal Academy of Arts, London

effect. The first public art exhibitions in 18th-century London show how some of contemporary art's institutionalised routines once came about. Fundamental conceptions of aesthetics and taste that emerged at the time were informed by their ideological context of Liberalism, British imperialism and the Scottish Enlightenment. On a material level, too, cultural production was intimately intertwined with colonial expropriation and class domination—through patronage and philanthropy. Together, these aspects played important parts in integrating constellations of dominance and imaginings of superiority into the core of European art institutions.

The development outlined—from the beginnings of art display in the Foundling Hospital to the first public exhibitions of contemporary art in London, and until the incorporation of The Society of Artists of Great Britain—demonstrates how, within two decades, the desires of a homogenous group of artists, all white men, were moulded into structures that defined how, for whom and under what conditions contemporary art entered the public sphere. The example therefore shows how artists' feelings became institutionalised and how the resulting organisations were, in addition, shaped by private economic and colonial interests. A wide spectrum of perspectives on contemporary art was prevented right from the start from participation, and thus the potential of a much broader art discourse precluded. Much about the structures created at that time closely resembles today's art institutions: donations solicited from individuals who make their money in highly problematic ways, collectors on boards shaping museum missions in line with their own interest, distinguished spheres and occasions to which only some are invited, a democratic *rhetoric* of openness to all people, combined with deterrents like high entrance fees, etc.

The art institution, as it emerged in this specific context, is a place where the desires and emotions of the socially dominant solidified into form. Exclusion and dominance, after all, are never matters only of cognition but also of affect. Inconvenience is a key term in this regard. The artists involved in the Society of Artists of Great Britain who hosted the first exhibitions felt inconvenienced particularly concerning two aspects. They expressed inconvenience in regard to spectators who they saw as intruders and who, in addition, dared to express their views, and to having their work exhibited alongside that of amateurs. In order to understand inconvenience as an affect in a public political sphere, Berlant's definition of "[i]nconvenience [as] the affective sense of the familiar friction of being in relation"[104] is helpful. Inconvenience reminds a subject that they are in relation, that they coexist, which constitutes a threat to their "sovereign fantasy":

At whatever scale and duration, "inconvenience" describes a feeling state that registers one's implication in the pressures of coexistence. [...] [T]his [...] kind of contact with inconvenience disturbs the vision of yourself you carry around that supports your sovereign fantasy, your fantasy of being in control. [...] [T]he sense of inconvenience of other people is evidence that no one was ever sovereign, just mostly operating according to some imaginable, often distorted image of their power over things, actions, people, and causality.[105]

When a sense of sovereignty is upset, this can be perceived as a disturbance, or even as a transgression of clearly imagined separations between subjects. The inconveniences lamented by the artists after their first exhibition in 1760 are a testament to the "friction of being in relation". When a public, which is addressed only as an abstract idea, shows up and behaves in unpredictable ways, this exposes the pressures of actual coexistence. The artists were made to register their being in relation with those audiences and amateur artists, whom they considered inferior. This caused friction with their self-conceptions, as well as with their aspiration to inscribe themselves into a new upper middle class. The perceived inconveniences of the artists were translated into new protocols for admission, demonstrating not only their desire for distinction, but also their adherence to a fantasy of sovereignty that experienced relation across difference as disruptive. The artists' relations to their "inconvenient audiences" were complicated, however, since their desired national fame depended on a public that needed to be addressed. Their conflicting sentiments and interests with regard to fame and exclusivity therefore produced an inescapable contradiction in which the broad public's attention was simultaneously desired and unwelcome. This closely echoes a passage from Berlant:

We know that, just by existing, historically subordinated populations are deemed inconvenient to the privileged who made

[104] Lauren Berlant, *On the Inconvenience of Other People* (Durham: Duke University Press, 2022), p. 2.

[105] Ibid., p. 3.

them so; the subordinated who are cast as a problem experience themselves as both necessary for and inconvenient to the general supremacist happiness.[106]

In many ways, this complex context of origin is the historical background against which to re-examine some normalised ideas that persist today in regard to artists and art institutions. Tracing the significant role that specific sentiments played in the institutionalisation of contemporary art means taking seriously the role of affect in its political dimensions, and perhaps helps to better recognise what remains of these sentiments in current structures. Contemporary art institutions today continue to be sites where several conflicting private and public desires meet. And often, they are characterised in a similar way by a democratic rhetoric that reflects their need for public support, both financial and symbolic, and simultaneous actions that devalue or exclude the public. Admission prices to publicly funded institutions today are often higher than what many people can afford to spend per day from their disposable income.[107] At the same time, audiences with looser ties to legitimised culture are targeted as desirable extensions to the institution's reach and impact. However, the prevailing restriction of access to art, its discourses and its concerns, has—not surprisingly—had a negative impact on public opinion. Therefore, the defunding of art institutions and education as witnessed over the last decades cannot be understood without taking into account contemporary art's longstanding history of elitism.

    As part of the genesis of the contemporary art institution discussed in this text, persons from a specific place and from particular subject positions shaped some of the procedures around art that were subsequently normalised as methods. The fact that in this context of origin dominance and exclusion were moulded into institutional form by artists upsets some core assumptions of various waves of institutional critique. The relation between artist and institution is often understood through the work of artist Andrea Fraser—one of the main practitioners of institutional critique—who claims that the artist acquires a position of privilege through institutional legitimisation, in which the artist then becomes the representative of the institution's authority. At the risk of simplification: once the artist enters the institution, the institution also enters the artist. This implies that the institution prior

[106] Lauren Berlant, *On the Inconvenience of Other People* (Durham: Duke University Press, 2022), p. 3.

[107] If there are days on which a general public can access exhibitions for free, admissions are often limited and special care is taken to protect the artworks from potential damage.

to these contaminations exists separately to the artist, who is envisioned as an actor wishing to transform the relations of the institution.[108]

The question is, however: is it really the artist who represents the institution's authority, or is it the institution that represents the artist's devastating desire for authority? While institutions have been problematised at depth, the figure of the artist has often been identified as a critical, subversive agent of change, who acts from an implicated position. As Marina Vishmidt puts it, "'Institutional critique' is retrospectively identified with a circular or, at best, enervatingly mimetic relation with the phantom antagonist/enabler (or enabling constraint) of the institution that is also 'in you' [...]."[109] This "phantom antagonist" described by Vishmidt derives from a problem inherent in critical practices that seek to put their object of critique at a distance, thereby making their own stakes in the problem difficult to grasp. The example of the Louvre, which was marked by statist principles and the representational interests of a new republic, provides such a setup for an oppositional positionality and for a "phantom antagonist". Here, the institution as a category can be conceived of as separate from the artist, even if they are entangled. By contrast, in the genesis described above of the contemporary art institutions in mid-18th century London, the artist appears not merely as a subject implicated in political and institutional forms of violence, but rather as an active agent in configuring art's material infrastructures. In this context, the longing for authority of a homogenous group of artists can be understood as the nucleus of the institution, which must therefore be regarded as the infrastructural materialisation of these dominant desires.

The detailed reconstruction of this context and the consideration of some of its effects are not intended as arguments for doing away with contemporary art, artists or art institutions, by presenting them as necessarily bad objects. To the contrary: if standard workings—some of which may seem self-evident and normal today—have, in fact, evolved in such improbable and sometimes absurdly petty ways, this makes it clear that things need not have unfolded in the way they did. Looking at this context of origin from 250 years ago so closely has, at least for me, made radical change easier to imagine. It has also brought about a series of questions. How to operate from a posture where the artist questions their

[108] See Andrea Fraser, 'An Artist's Statement', in *Museum Highlights: The Writings of Andrea Fraser*, edited by Alexander Alberro (Cambridge, Massachusetts: MIT Press, 2005), pp. 44–45.

[109] Marina Vishmidt, 'Between Not Everything and Not Nothing: Cuts Toward Infrastructural Critique' (Cambridge, Massachusetts: MIT Press, 2017), p. 265.

own stakes within exclusionary mechanisms? How to institute better? Apart from admission fees, what else is normalised in today's notions and routines around art, so that the violence within it can easily go unregistered? How to be attentive to the many subtle and mundane ways in which dominance operates? What is the role of compassion today when the suffering and genocidal killings of people are increasingly being rationalised as necessary? Whose voices cause inconvenience? How to dismantle structures put in place only to protect from necessary inconveniences? Can inconvenience "become a resource for building solidarity and alliance across ambivalence, rather than appearing mainly as the negative sandpaper of sociality?"[110]

[110] Lauren Berlant, *On the Inconvenience of Other People* (2022), p. 8.

Vika Kirchenbauer

Compassion and Inconvenience

Single-channel video,
30:00, 2024

By *JOHN GWYNN.*

LONDON and WESTMINSTER
IMPROVED,
ILLUSTRATED by PLANS.

To which is prefixed,

A Difcourfe on Publick Magnificence;

WITH

Obfervations on the State of Arts and Artifts in this
Kingdom, wherein the Study of the Polite Arts
is recommended as neceffary to a liberal Education:

By *JOHN GWYNN.*

1766

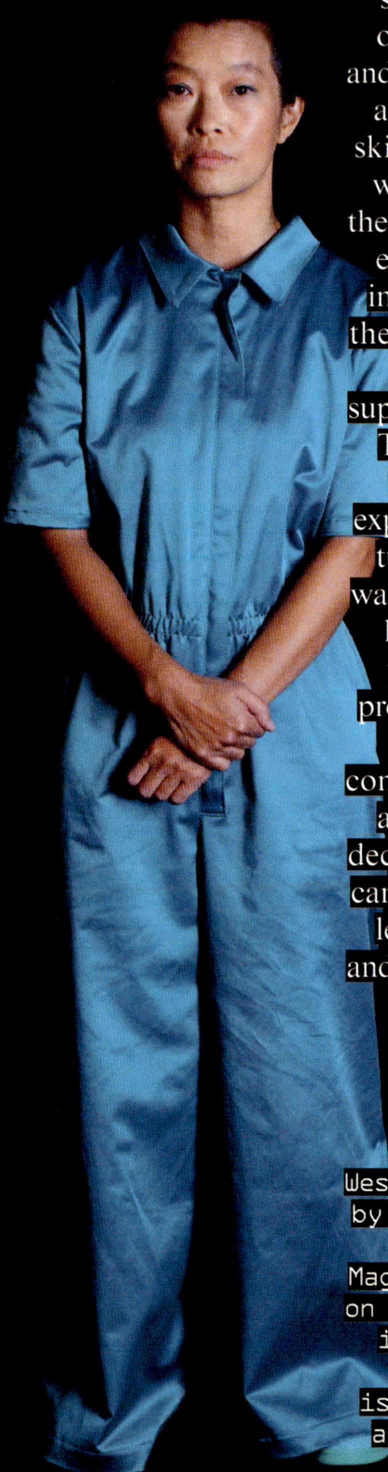

Suppose a colony of emigrants first settling in any climate, the calls of nature are few. Building huts, and tillage, are the first objects of their attention; and their cloathing the skins of beasts. These supply them with food, and defend them from the inclemencies of the seasons, until encreasing in numbers, and their improvements advancing equally, their lands produce more than they consume, and they are able to supply the wants of their neighbours. This introduces commerce and navigation. The demands for exportation stimulate the manufacturer, wealth arises, and artificial wants encrease; the rich inhabitants look out for the means of ease, pleasure and distinction; these produce the polite arts, and the original formation of huts is now converted into architecture; painting and sculpture contribute to the decoration, and stamp that value on canvas and marble which is acknowledged by taste and discernment and mark those necessary distinctions between the palace and the cottage.[1]

1
John Gwynn, London and Westminster Improved, Illustrated by Plans to which is prefixed, A Discourse on Publick Magnificence, with Observations on the State of Arts and Artists in this Kingdom, wherein the Study of the Polite Arts is recommended as Necessary to a Liberal Education (London: 1766), pp. xiii–xiv.

Compaſſion *and* *Inconvenience*

[Monotonous hum]

VIKA KIRCHENBAUER

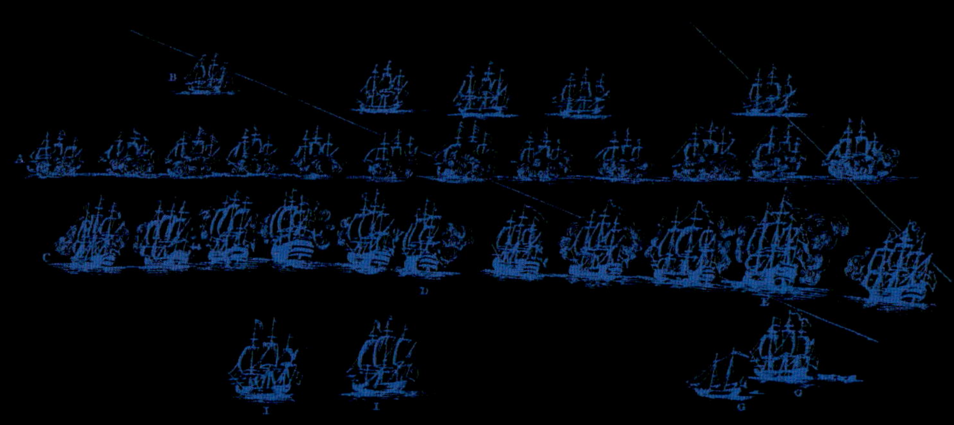

[Waves splash]

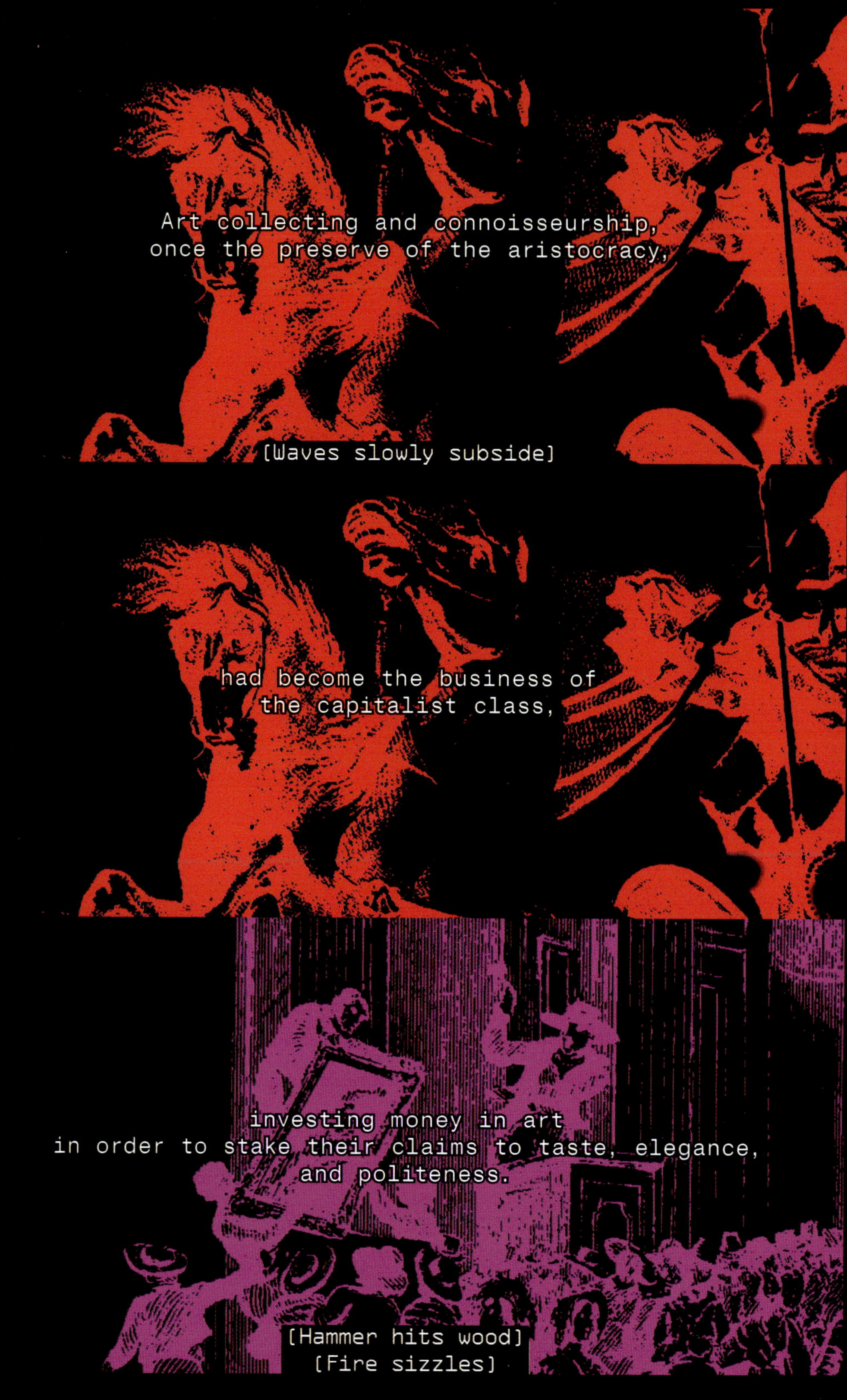

Art collecting and connoisseurship,
once the preserve of the aristocracy,
[Waves slowly subside]
had become the business of
the capitalist class,
investing money in art
in order to stake their claims to taste, elegance,
and politeness.
[Hammer hits wood]
[Fire sizzles]

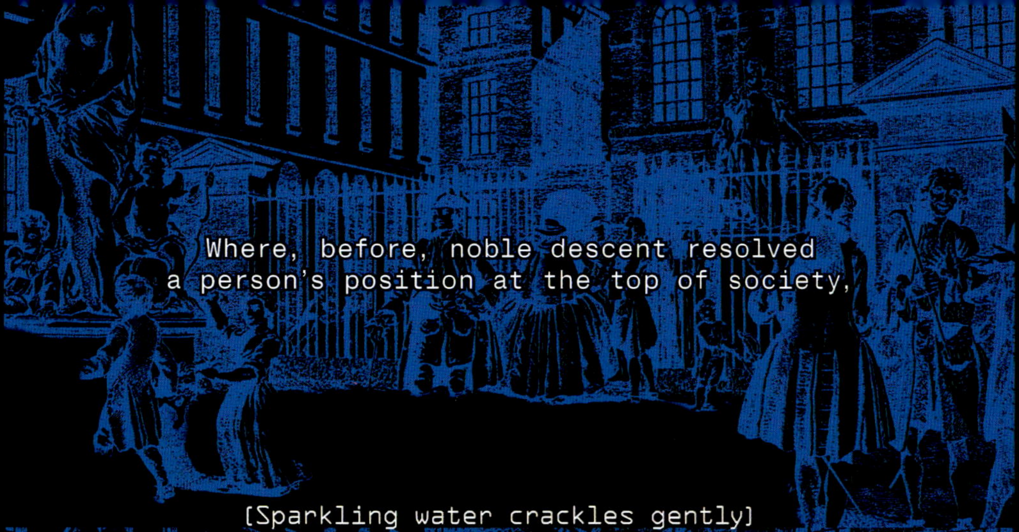

Where, before, noble descent resolved
a person's position at the top of society,

[Sparkling water crackles gently]

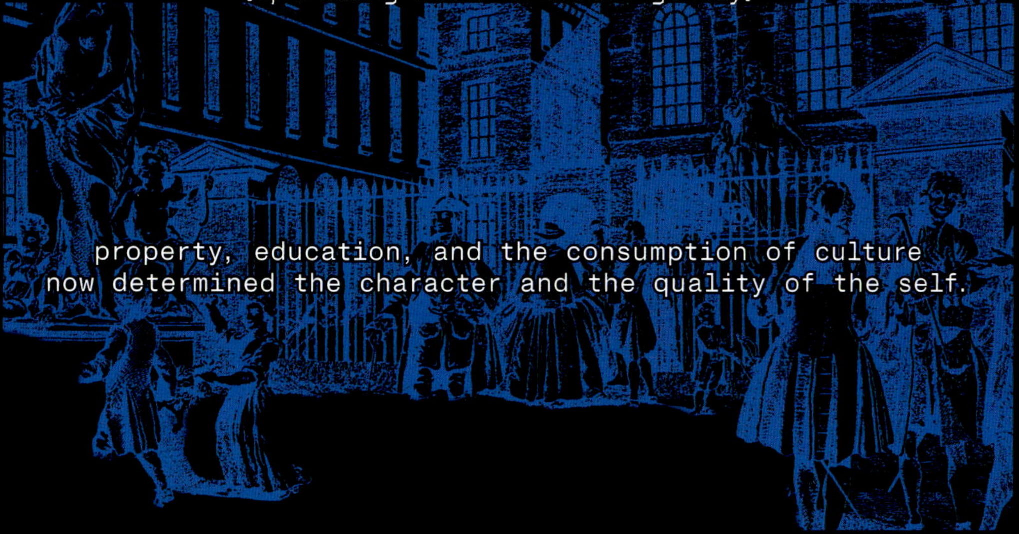

property, education, and the consumption of culture
now determined the character and the quality of the self.

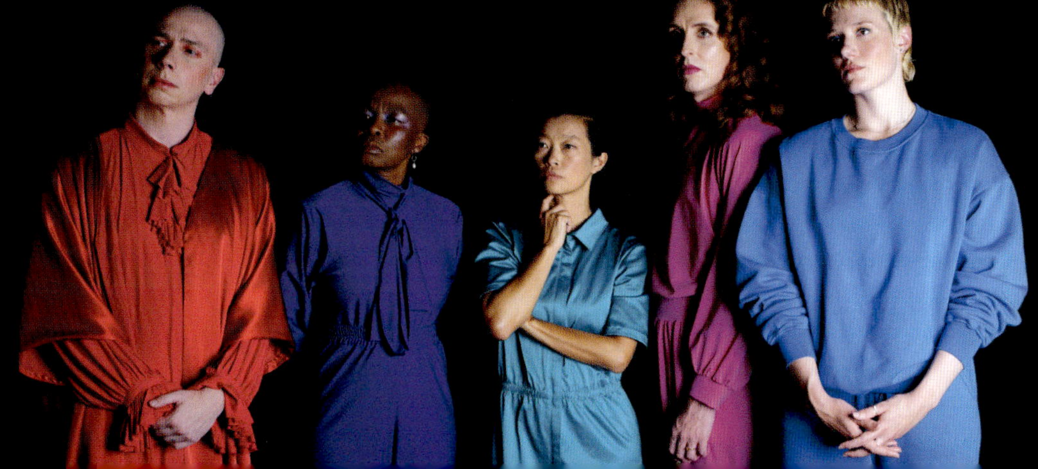

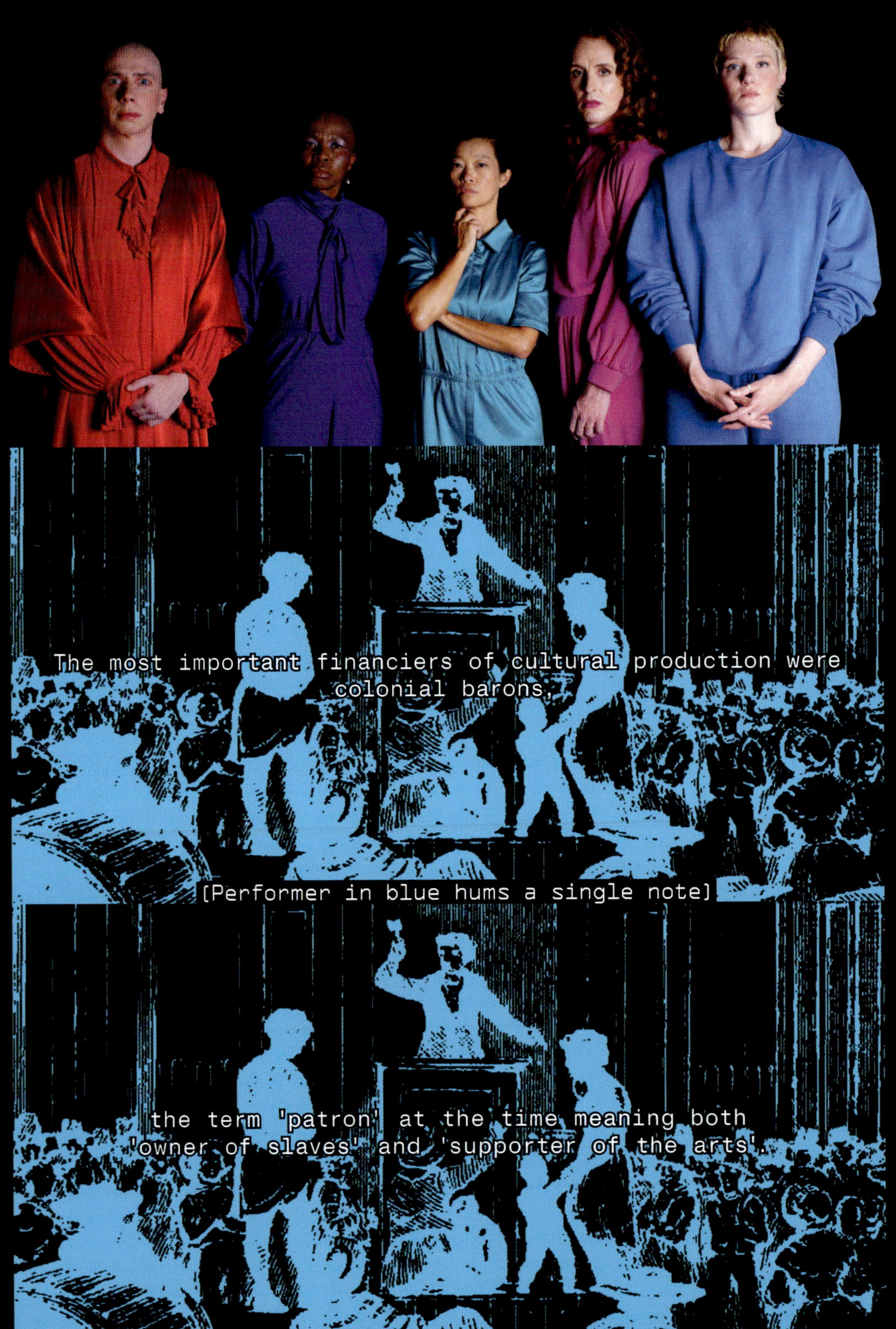
The most important financiers of cultural production were
colonial barons,
[Performer in blue hums a single note]
the term 'patron' at the time meaning both
'owner of slaves' and 'supporter of the arts'.

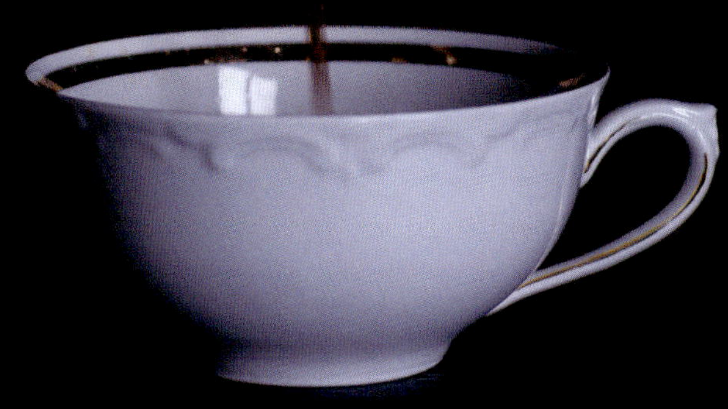

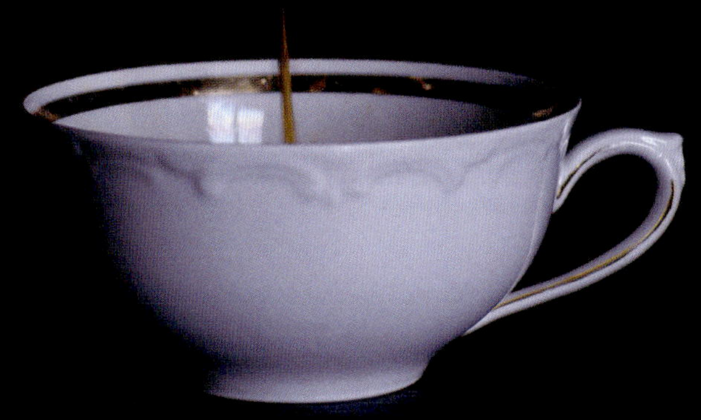

A

TREATISE

ON

ANCIENT PAINTING,

By GEORGE TURNBULL

1740

MK:
What is it that gives either Grace, or Dignity, or Relish to human Life, but the ingenious Arts? What else is it that raises Society to true Grandeur? Take away the Virtues and Arts, and what remains but merely sensual and animal Gratifications? What remains that is peculiar to Man, that exalts him above the groveling Brutes, or intitles a Society of Men to the Character of a Rational Society?[2]

Our Eyes and Ears, says *Cicero*, are superior to those of the Brutes; because there is in our Minds a Sense of Beauty and Harmony in sensible Objects, by means of which these outward Senses may be improved into Instruments, or rather Ministers, of several beautiful, highly entertaining Arts.[3]

[2]
George Turnbull, *A Treatise on Ancient Painting, Containing Observations on the Rise, Progress, and Decline of that Art amongst the Greeks and Romans* (London: Printed for the author, and sold by A. Millar, 1740), p. 122.
[3]
Ibid., p. 142.

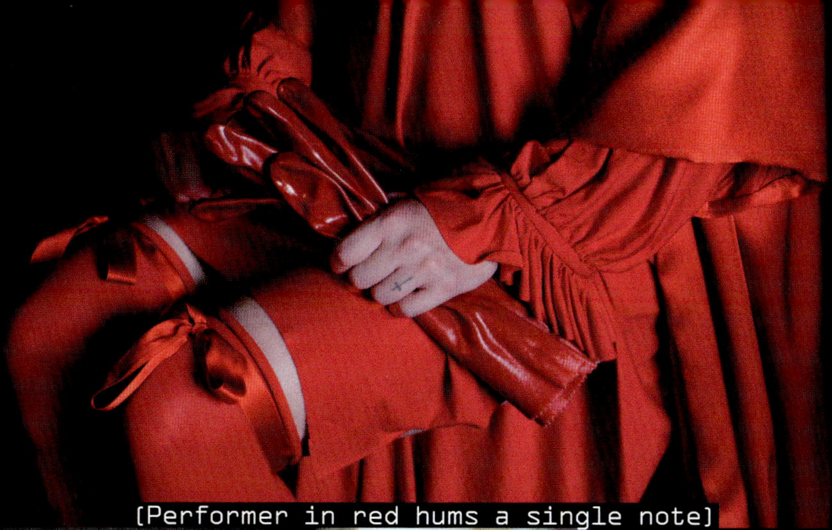

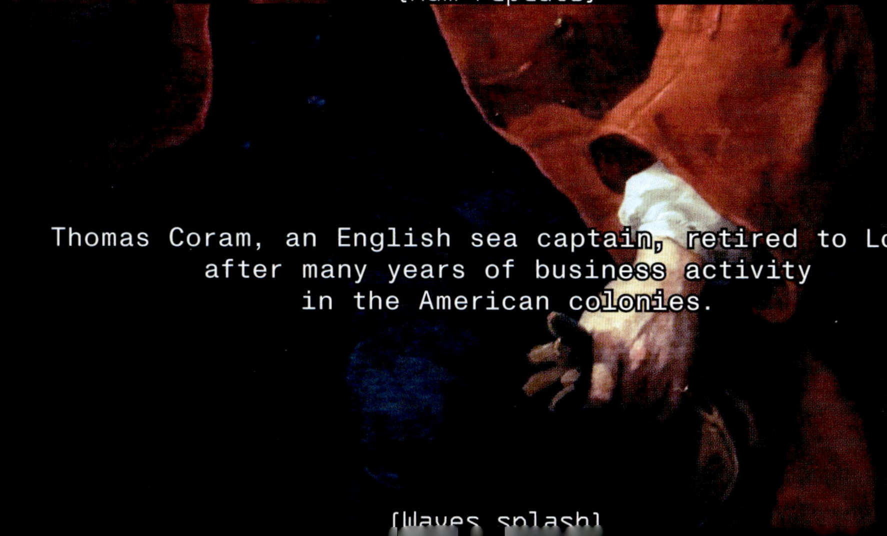

Thomas Coram, an English sea captain, retired to London
after many years of business activity
in the American colonies.

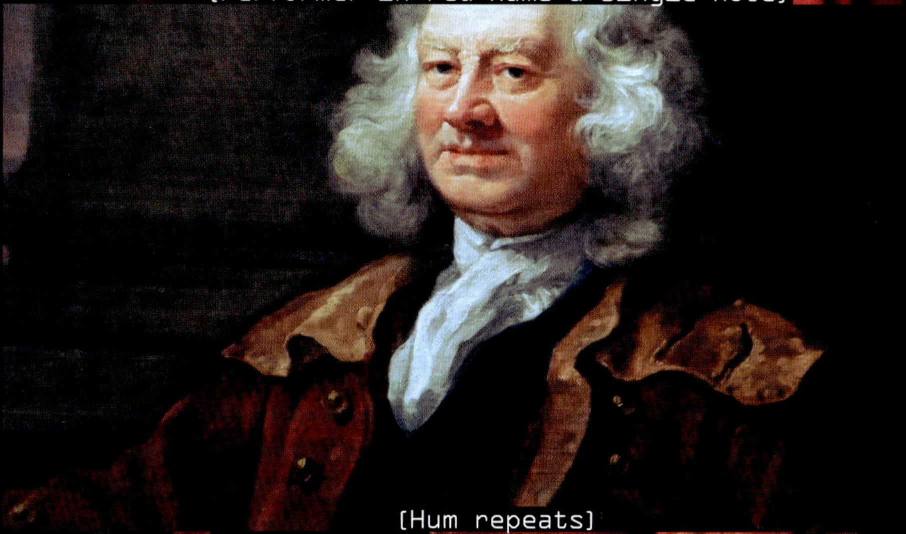

In the colonies, the life of a
white child was of great value to the settlers.

[Splashing continues]

In London, it was common to witness
destitute and dying children on the streets.

[Wind blows]

Child mortality rates were so high that
the capitalist class was alarmed that
the country would simply run out of
the sailors, soldiers, servants, maids and labourers
necessary to secure their wealth.

[Siren-line hum sets in]
[Ship's bell sounds]

Abſtract of the *London* WEEKLY
BILL, from *Aug.* 29. to *Sept.* 26. 1732.

Chriſtned { Males   670 } 1278
          { Females 608 }

Buried   { Males   973 } 1927
          { Females 954 }

Died under 2 Years old   944
Between   2   and   5   129

[Eerie hum continues]

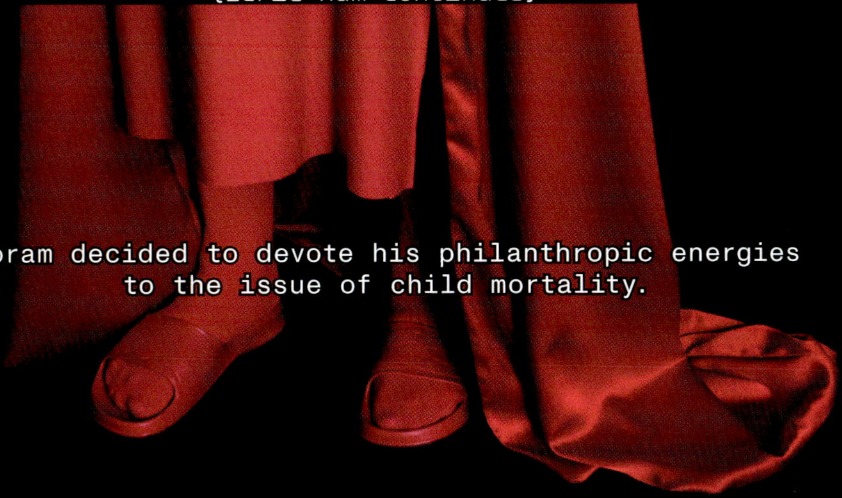

Coram decided to devote his philanthropic energies
to the issue of child mortality.

[Hum slowly fades]

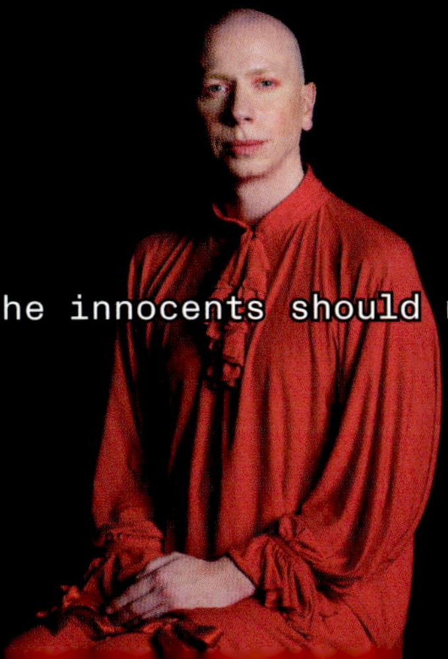

So that the innocents should no longer be

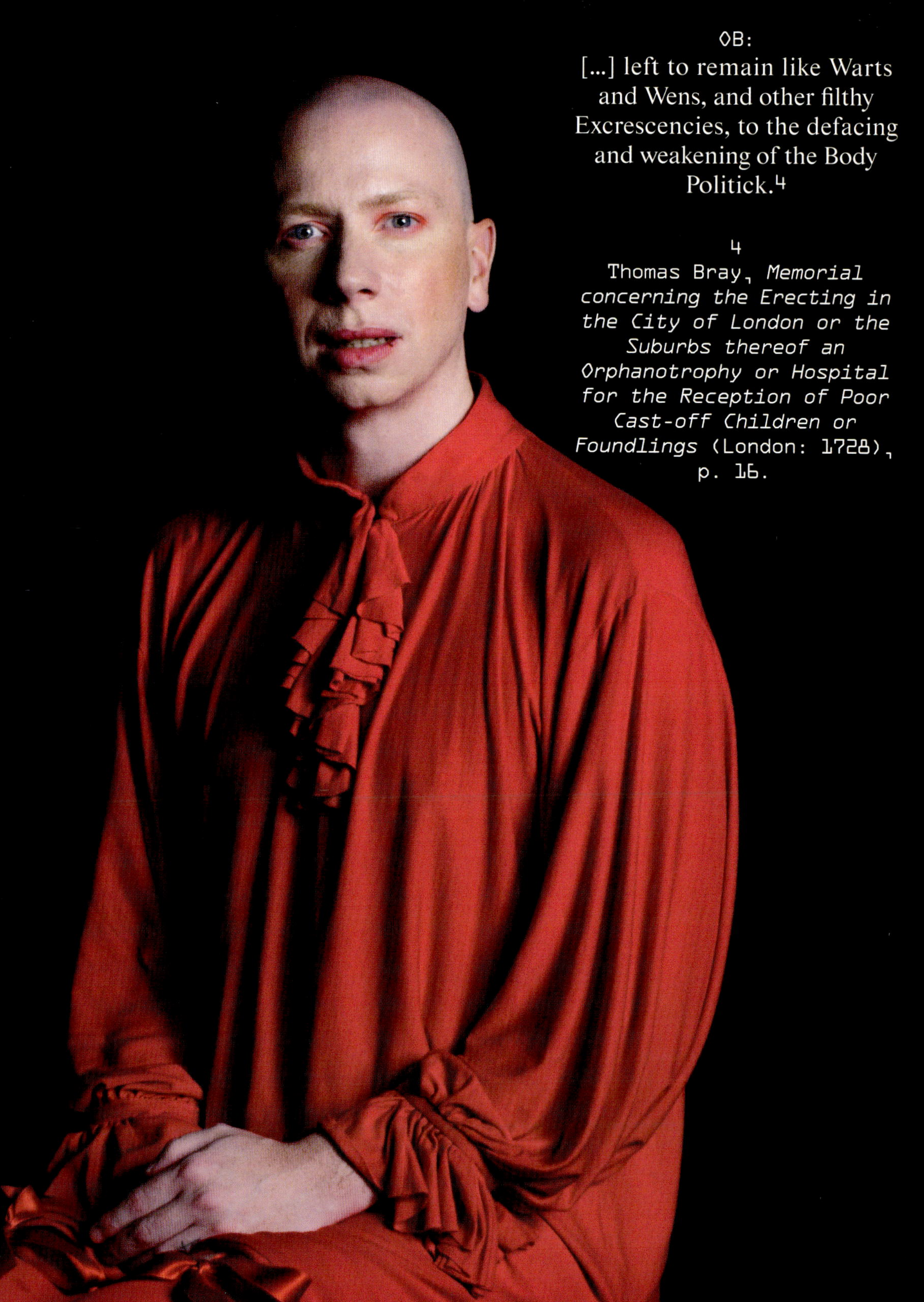
OB:
[...] left to remain like Warts
and Wens, and other filthy
Excrescencies, to the defacing
and weakening of the Body
Politick.4

4
Thomas Bray, Memorial
concerning the Erecting in
the City of London or the
Suburbs thereof an
Orphanotrophy or Hospital
for the Reception of Poor
Cast-off Children or
Foundlings (London: 1728),
p. 16.

George the Second by the Grace of
God & so forth To All to whome these Presents
shall come Greeting Whereas our Trusty and
Welbeloved Subject Thomas Coram Gentleman
in behalf of Great Numbers of helpless Infants
daily exposed to Destruction has by his Petition
humbly represented Unto Us that many Persons
of Quality & Distinction as well as others of
both Sexes (being Sensible of the frequent
Murders committed on poor Miserable Infants by

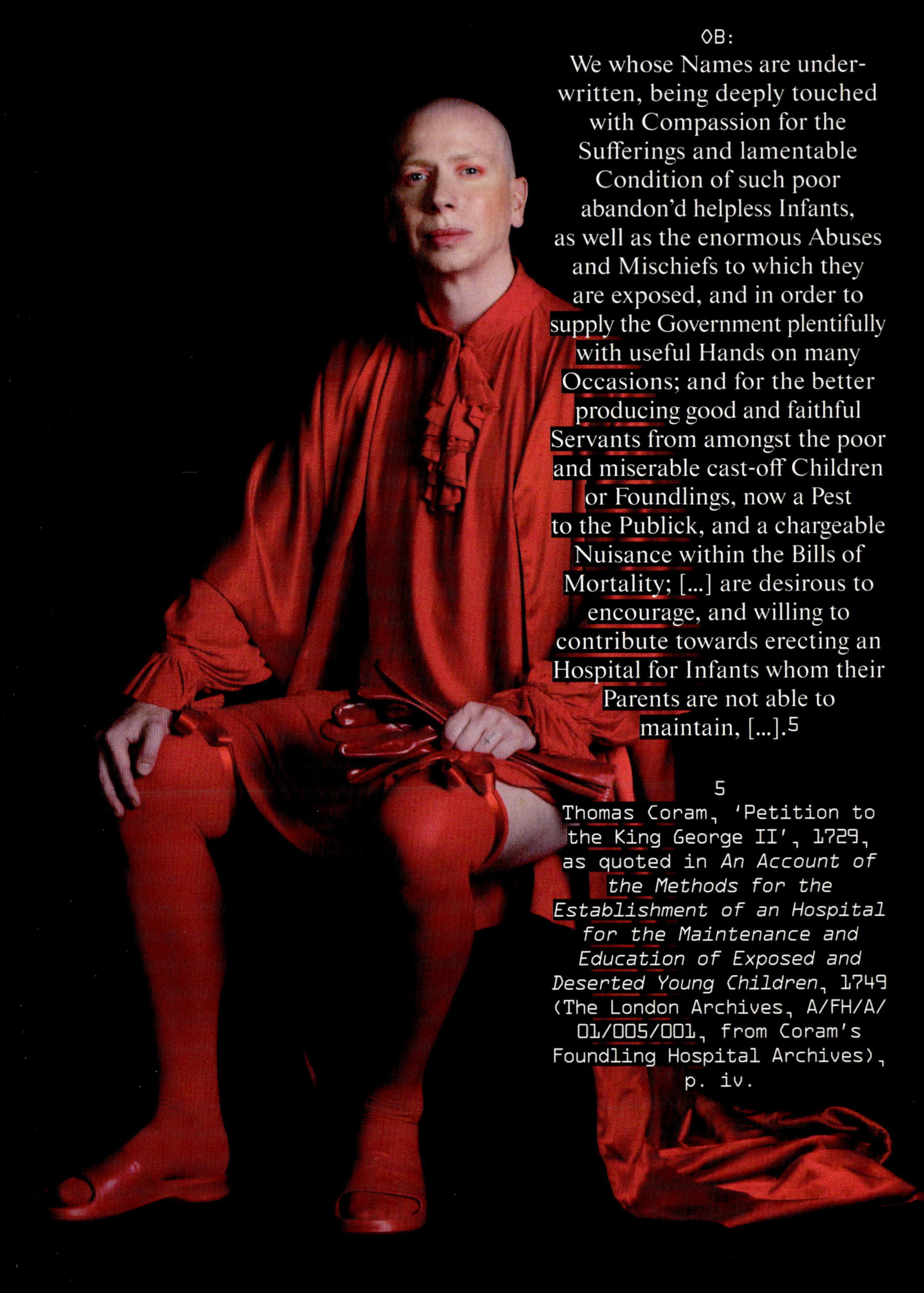

We whose Names are under-
written, being deeply touched
with Compassion for the
Sufferings and lamentable
Condition of such poor
abandon'd helpless Infants,
as well as the enormous Abuses
and Mischiefs to which they
are exposed, and in order to
supply the Government plentifully
with useful Hands on many
Occasions; and for the better
producing good and faithful
Servants from amongst the poor
and miserable cast-off Children
or Foundlings, now a Pest
to the Publick, and a chargeable
Nuisance within the Bills of
Mortality; [...] are desirous to
encourage, and willing to
contribute towards erecting an
Hospital for Infants whom their
Parents are not able to
maintain, [...].[5]

5
Thomas Coram, 'Petition to the King George II', 1729, as quoted in *An Account of the Methods for the Establishment of an Hospital for the Maintenance and Education of Exposed and Deserted Young Children*, 1749 (The London Archives, A/FH/A/01/005/001, from Coram's Foundling Hospital Archives), p. iv.

◊B:
Most humbley Sheweth
That many Ladys of Quality
and Distinction being deeply touched
with Concern for the frequent
Murders committed on poor Miserable
Infant Children at their Birth by
their Cruel Parents to hide their Shame
and for the Inhumane Custom of
exposing Newborn Children to Perish
in the Streets or the putting out of
such unhappy Foundlings to wicked and
barbarous Nurses who [...] turn them
into the Streets to begg or steal [...],
and some of those Miserable Infants are
Blinded or Maimed or Distorted
in their Limbs in order to move Pity &
Compassion and thereby become the
fitter Instruments of gain to those
Vile, Mercyless Wretches. [...]
[A] Foundation [...] Established under
good Management would not only save
the lives of Many of your Majesties
Subjects but be a Meanes of rendering
them useful to the Publick either
in the Sea or Land Service [...] [A]
Designe so humane and Charitable as
rescuing helpless Infants from
inevitable Destruction cannot fail of
being Encouraged by many Rich well
disposed persons [...].6

6
Thomas Coram, 'The Memorial &
Petition of Thomas Coram Gent.
in behalf of great numbers of
Helpless Infants daily exposed to
Destruction', 1737, as quoted
in Herbert Fuller Bright Compston,
*Thomas Coram, Churchman, Empire
Builder, and Philanthropist*
(London: Society for Promoting
Christian Knowledge, 1918),
pp. 89–91.

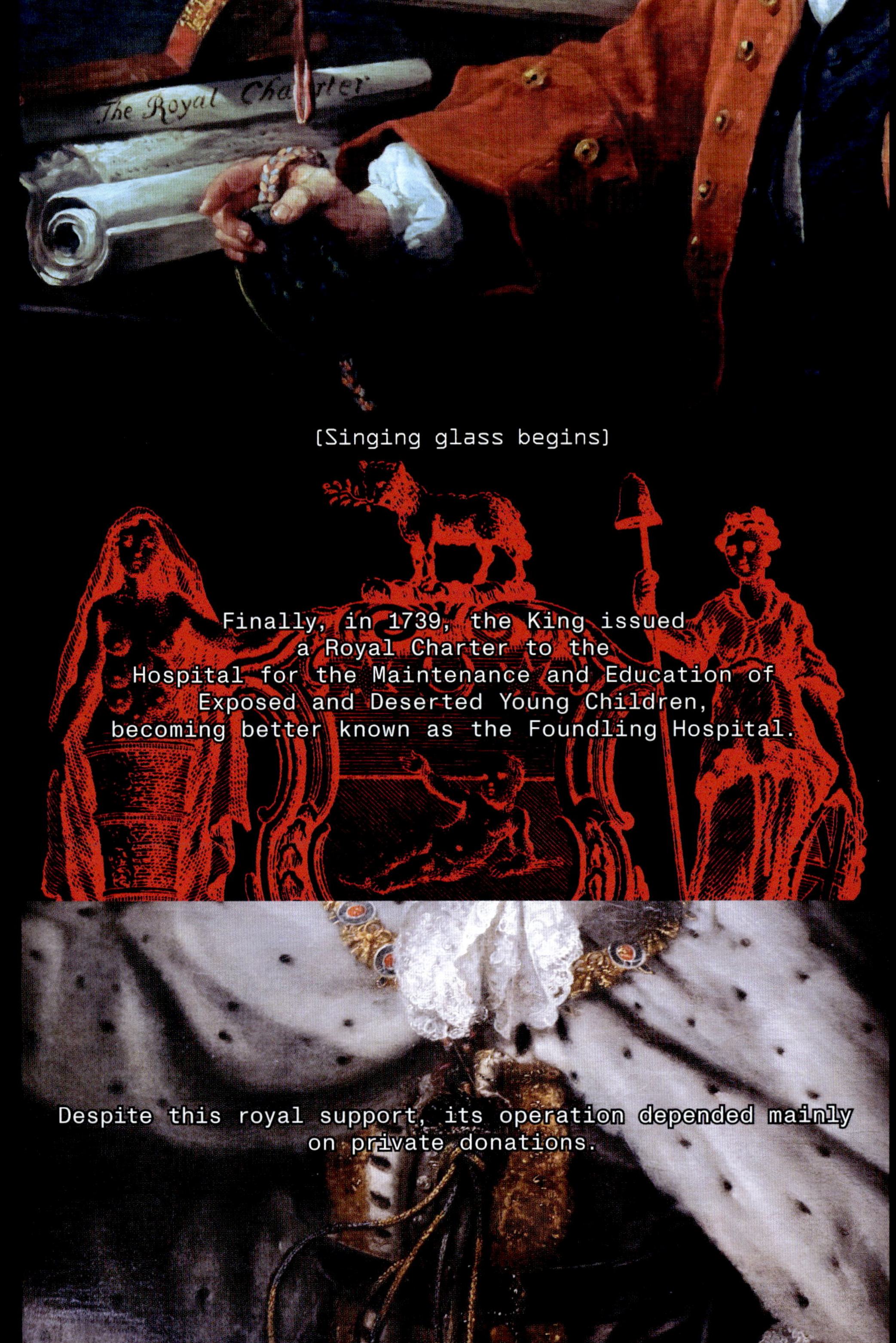
The Royal Charter
[Singing glass begins]
Finally, in 1739, the King issued
a Royal Charter to the
Hospital for the Maintenance and Education of
Exposed and Deserted Young Children,
becoming better known as the Foundling Hospital.
Despite this royal support, its operation depended mainly
on private donations.

In order to attract donors, it was decided to include
in the building a picture gallery,
with paintings depicting biblical scenes of charity.

[Singing glass continues]

The institution had to be
a facility of education to the poor,
and a site of refined entertainment to the wealthy.

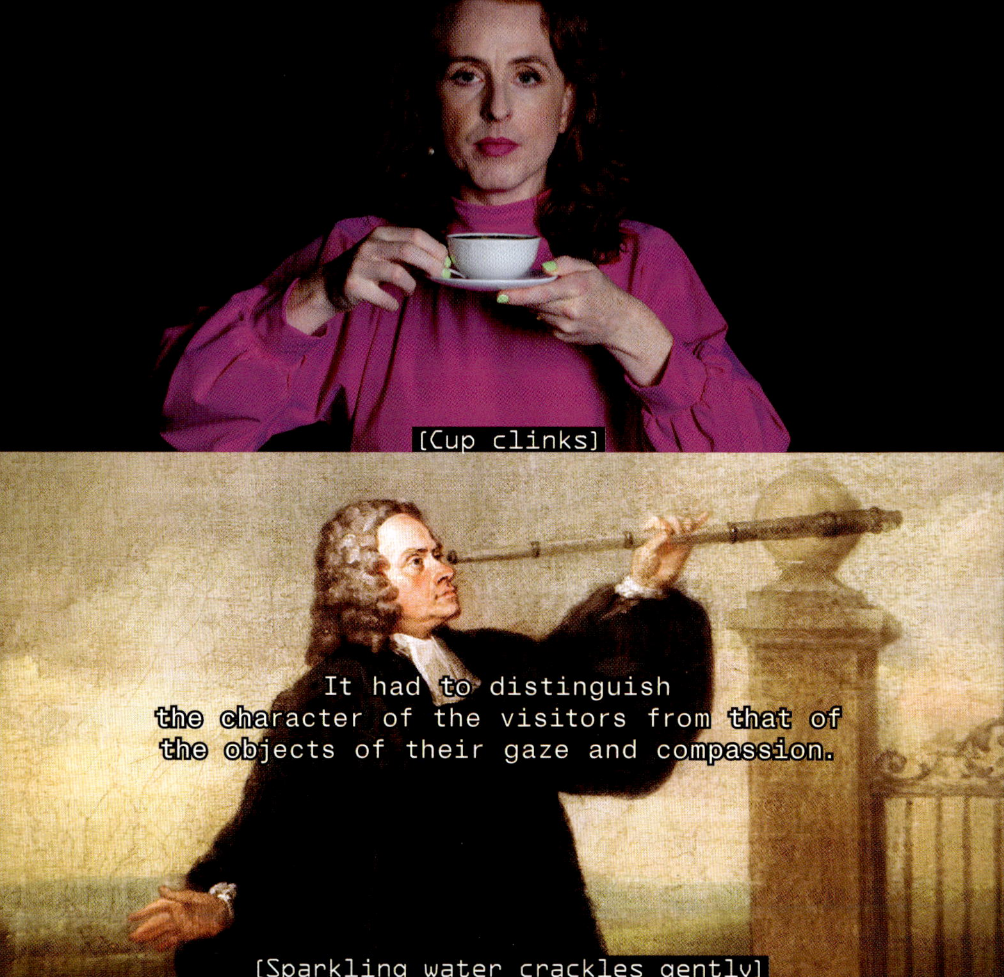

[Cup clinks]
It had to distinguish
the character of the visitors from that of
the objects of their gaze and compassion.
[Sparkling water crackles gently]

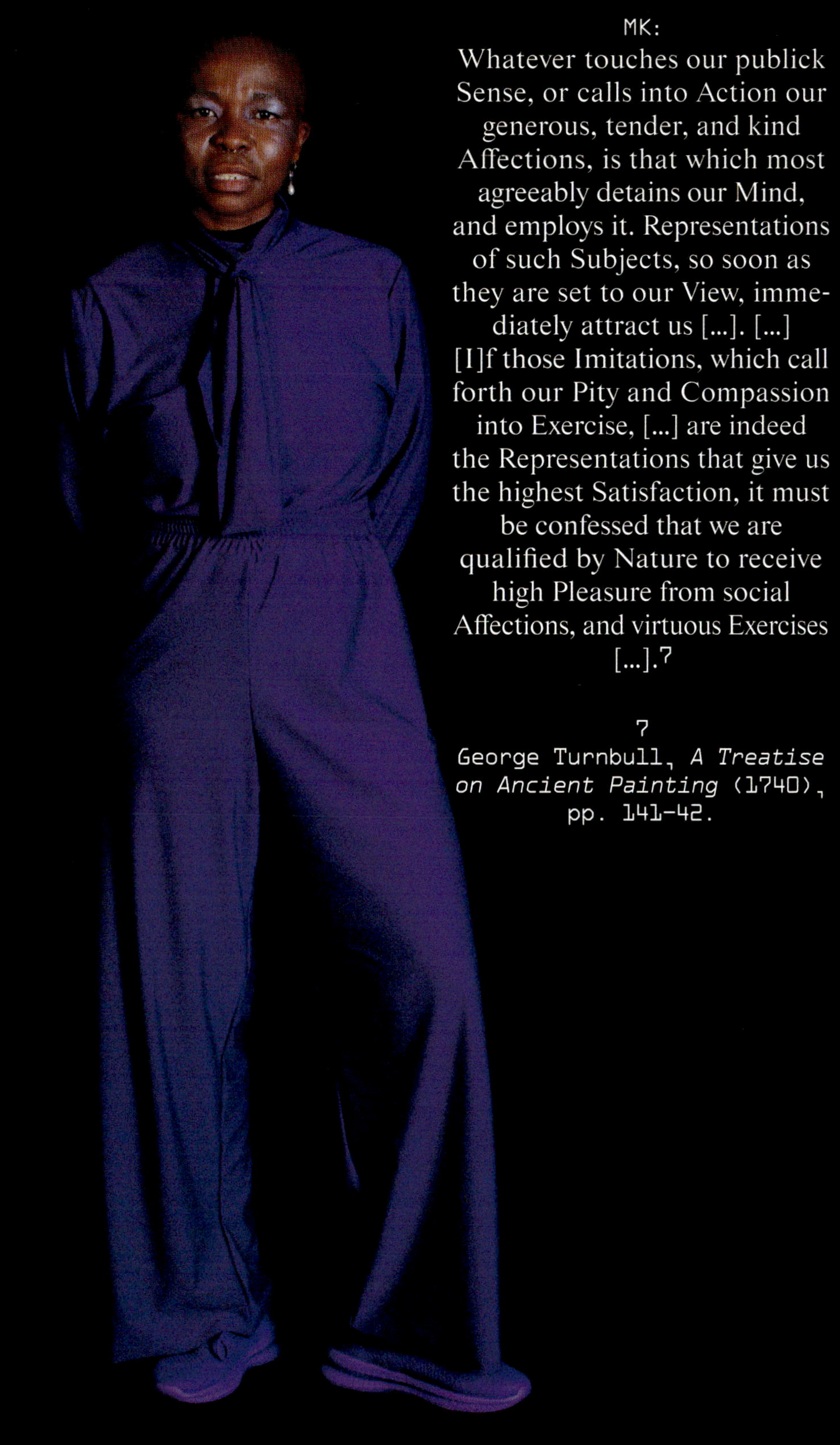

MK:
Whatever touches our publick
Sense, or calls into Action our
generous, tender, and kind
Affections, is that which most
agreeably detains our Mind,
and employs it. Representations
of such Subjects, so soon as
they are set to our View, imme-
diately attract us [...]. [...]
[I]f those Imitations, which call
forth our Pity and Compassion
into Exercise, [...] are indeed
the Representations that give us
the highest Satisfaction, it must
be confessed that we are
qualified by Nature to receive
high Pleasure from social
Affections, and virtuous Exercises
[...].7

7
George Turnbull, A Treatise
on Ancient Painting (1740),
pp. 141-42.

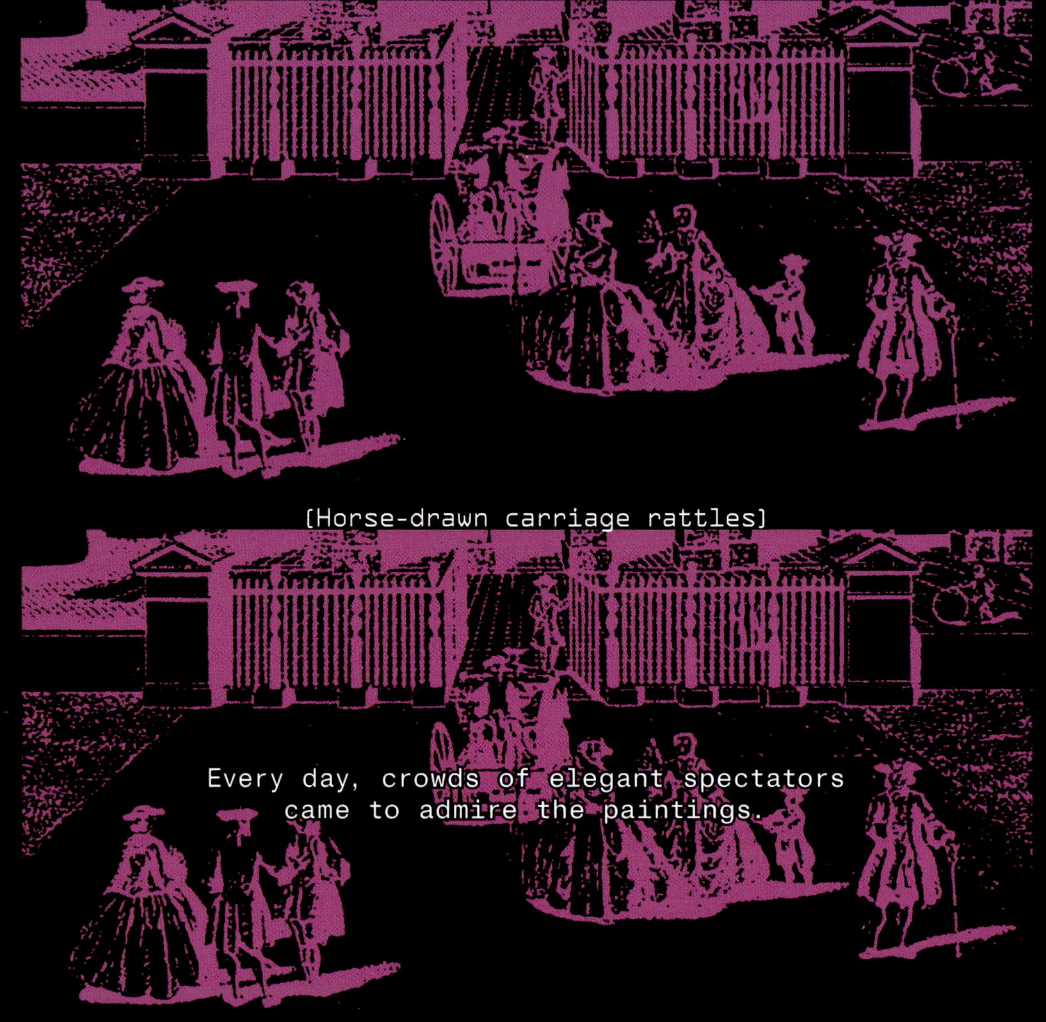
[Horse-drawn carriage rattles]
Every day, crowds of elegant spectators
came to admire the paintings.
The poor foundlings, presented in their uniforms,
were no less of an attraction.

Situated in open fields beyond the confines of the city,

here the donors could mingle with other members
of their class, and observe the impact
of their benevolence.

[Performer in blue hums a sustained note]

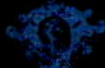

How selfish soever man may be
supposed, there are evidently some
principles in his nature, which
interest him in the fortune of others,
and render their happiness
necessary to him, though he derives
nothing from it except the pleasure
of seeing it. Of this kind is pity
and compassion, the emotion which
we feel for the misery of others,
when we either see it, or are made to
conceive it in a very lively manner.[8]

First of all, our sympathy with sorrow
is, in some sense, more universal than
that with joy. [...]
Pain [...], whether of mind or body,
is a more pungent sensation than
pleasure, and our sympathy with pain,
though it falls greatly short of
what is naturally felt by the sufferer,
is generally a more lively and
distinct perception than our sympathy
with pleasure [...].[9]

The compassion of the spectator
must arise altogether from the
consideration of what he himself
would feel if he was reduced to
the same unhappy situation, and,
what perhaps is impossible, was at
the same time able to regard it with
his present reason and judgment.[10]

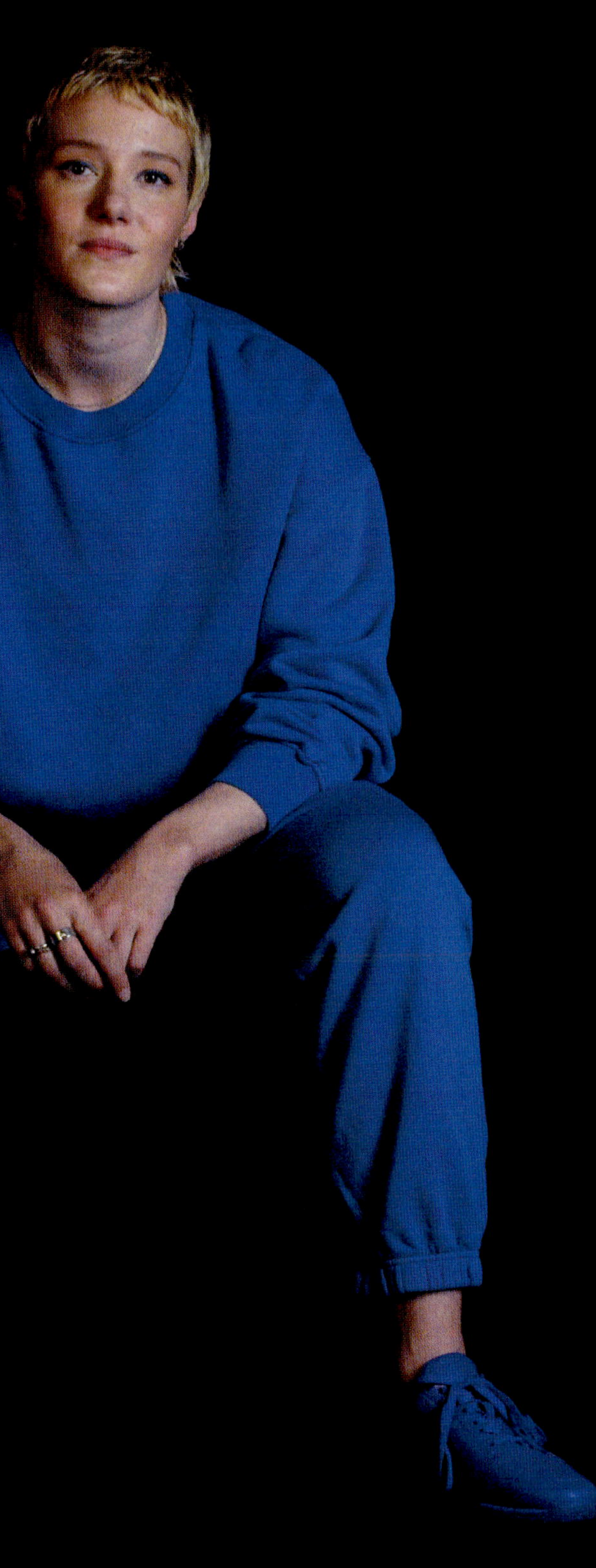

---

[8]
Adam Smith, *The Theory of Moral
Sentiments* (London: Printed
for A. Millar and A. Kincaid
and J. Bell, 1759), pp. 1-2.
[9]
Ibid., pp. 94-95.
[10]
Ibid., p. 10.

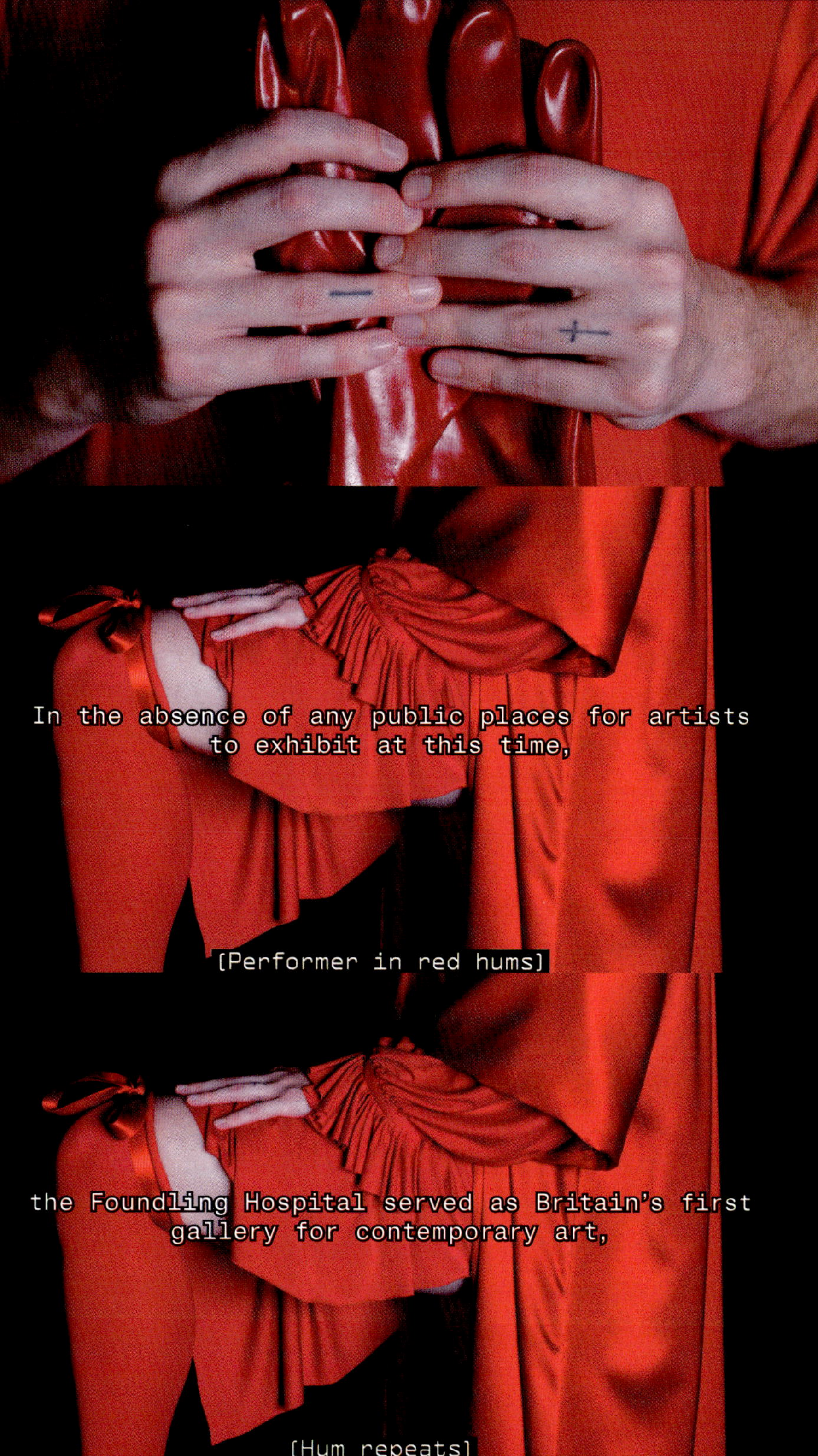

In the absence of any public places for artists
to exhibit at this time,

[Performer in red hums]

the Foundling Hospital served as Britain's first
gallery for contemporary art,

[Hum repeats]

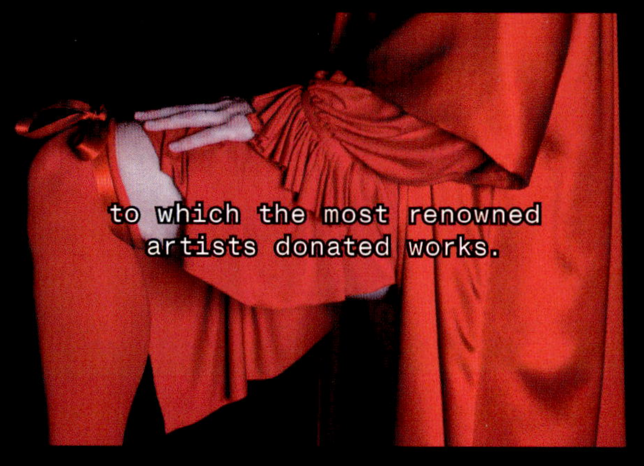

to which the most renowned
artists donated works.

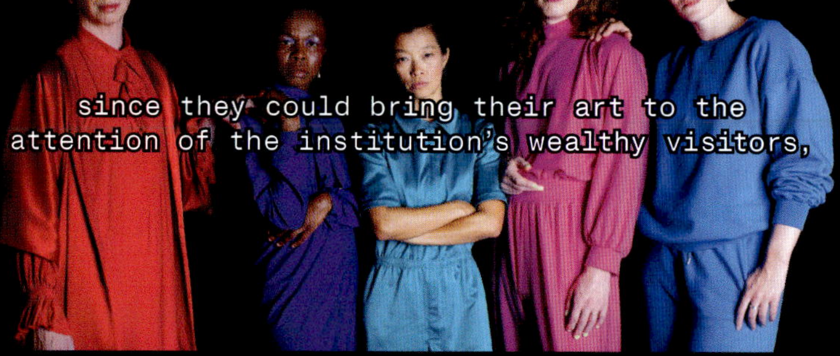

The artists saw in this an opportunity for patronage,

since they could bring their art to the
attention of the institution's wealthy visitors,

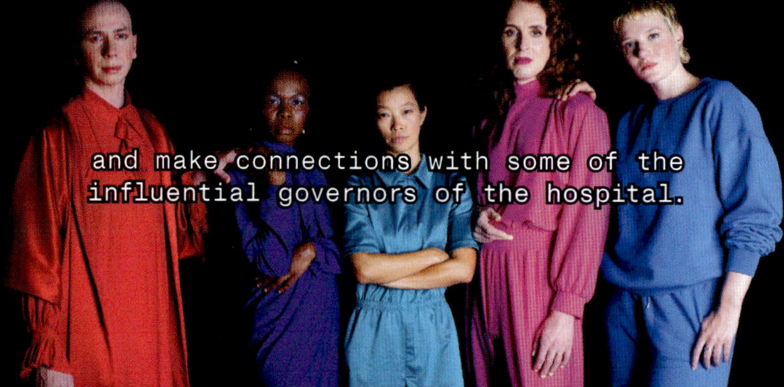

and make connections with some of the
influential governors of the hospital.

Many of the governors were colonial barons
who resided overseas.

Wealthy sugar planters and slavers were
among the institution's biggest donors.

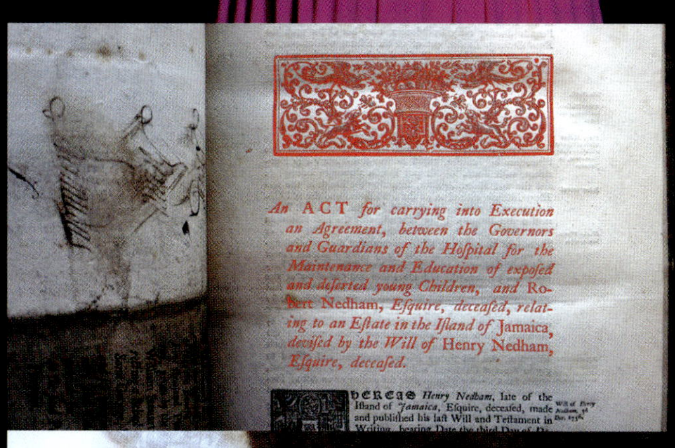

From such supporters it inherited
plantations and estates,
at times explicitly including the enslaved people
on the land, as well as their future offspring.

several Outhouses Works Buildings Woodland and other La[nds]
Rights Members and Appurtenances And likewise All tha[t]
the name of Woodstock plantation Together with the pre[...]
Hereditaments thereto belonging and the Rights Member[s]
are situate in the Parish of Saint Ann in the said Island
walk with the Capital Messuage or Mansion House th[...]
or thereunto appertaining with all woods woodlands and
Williams deceased situate in the Parish of Saint James i[...]
all and every the Negro Mulatto and other Slaves whatso[ever]
and future Issue Offspring or increase And all other the
devised or bequeath to or for the use of them the said
Williams deceased To have and to hold the said [...]
Messuages Lands Woods Woodlands Tenements and Heredit[aments]
promises herein before mentioned or intended to be barga[ined]
of their Rights Members and Appurtenances unto the said [...]

The hospital leased and sold these to fund its operation.

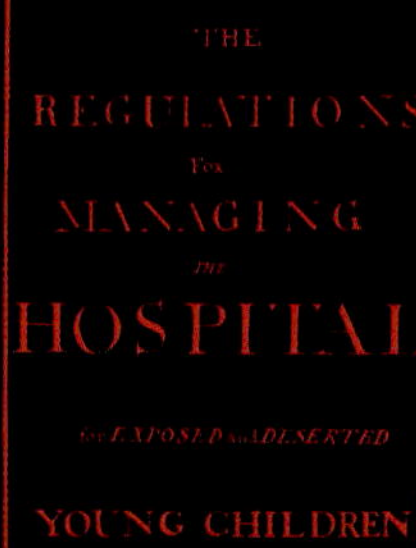

OB:
The Children are to be put
out as soon as possible to the
Business, for which they are
appointed [...]. [...] It is hoped
that [...] an order may be
obtained from the Lords of the
Admiralty to the Captains of
His Majesty's Ships to take
a certain Number of Boys [...],
and if the Captain of every
Merchant Ship [...] was obliged
[...] to take one or more
it would greatly Increase the
Number of Seamen [...].
[T]he Girls are to be placed out
as Household Servants or put
out for a Term of years to be employed in the Linnen or
Woolen Manufactory as soon
as possible [...].[11]

[11]
'The Methods of Placing them
out to proper Employments',
in *The Regulations for
Managing the Hospital for
Exposed and Deserted Young
Children*, 1742 (TLA:
A/FH/A/06/015/001, from
Coram's Foundling Hospital
Archives).

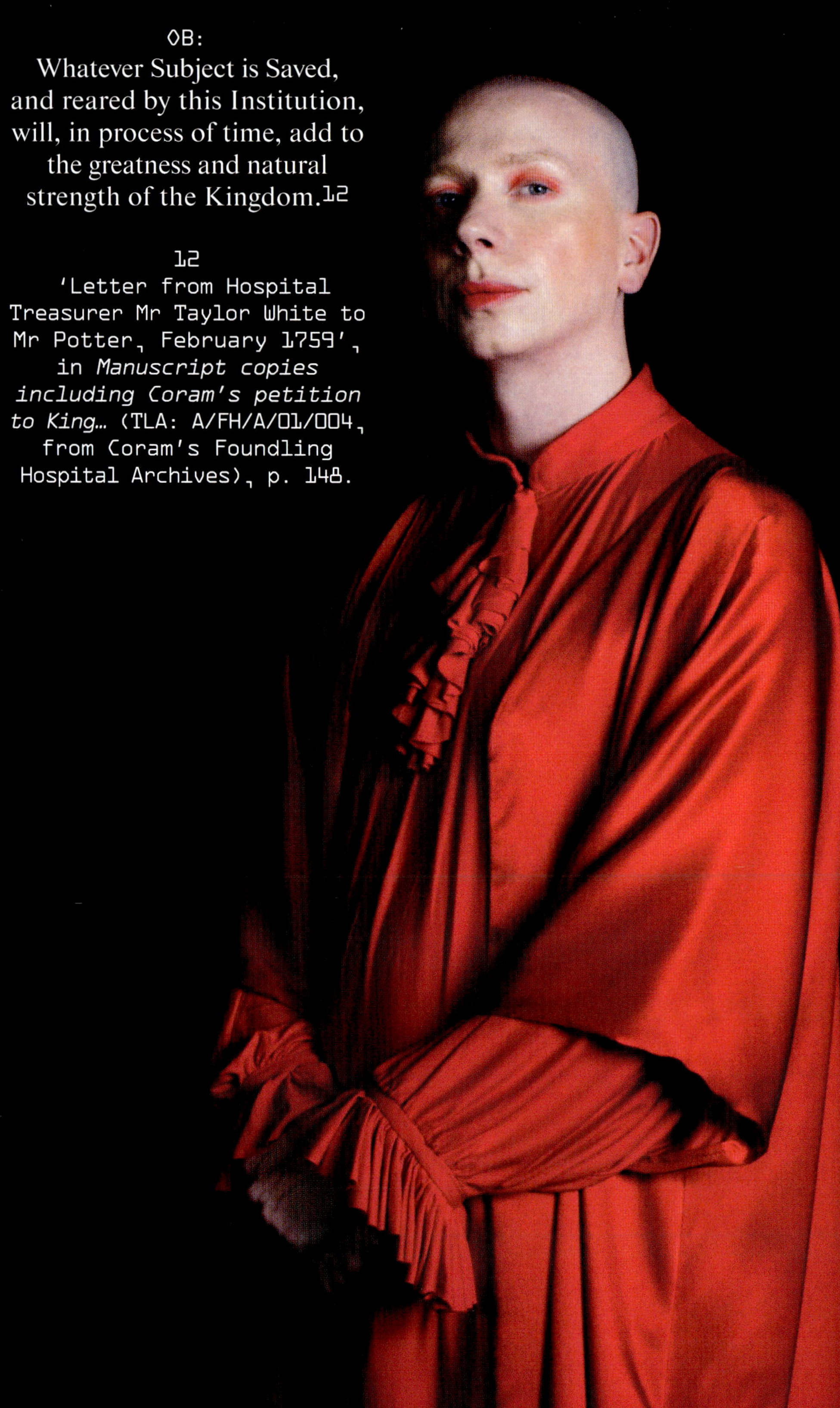

OB:
Whatever Subject is Saved,
and reared by this Institution,
will, in process of time, add to
the greatness and natural
strength of the Kingdom.12

12
'Letter from Hospital
Treasurer Mr Taylor White to
Mr Potter, February 1759',
in Manuscript copies
including Coram's petition
to King... (TLA: A/FH/A/01/004,
from Coram's Foundling
Hospital Archives), p. 148.

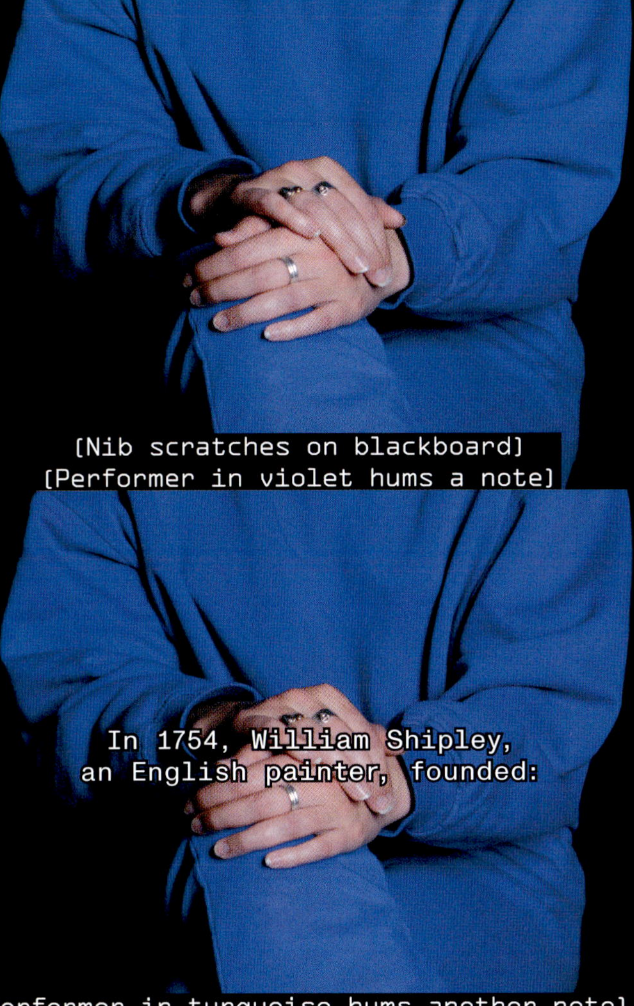

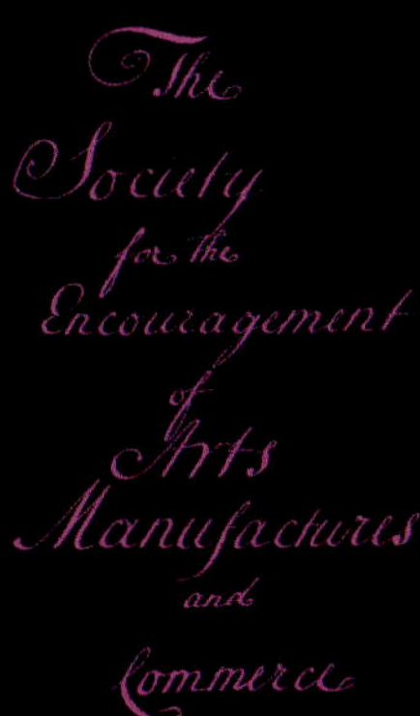

[Performer in pink joins in, off-key]

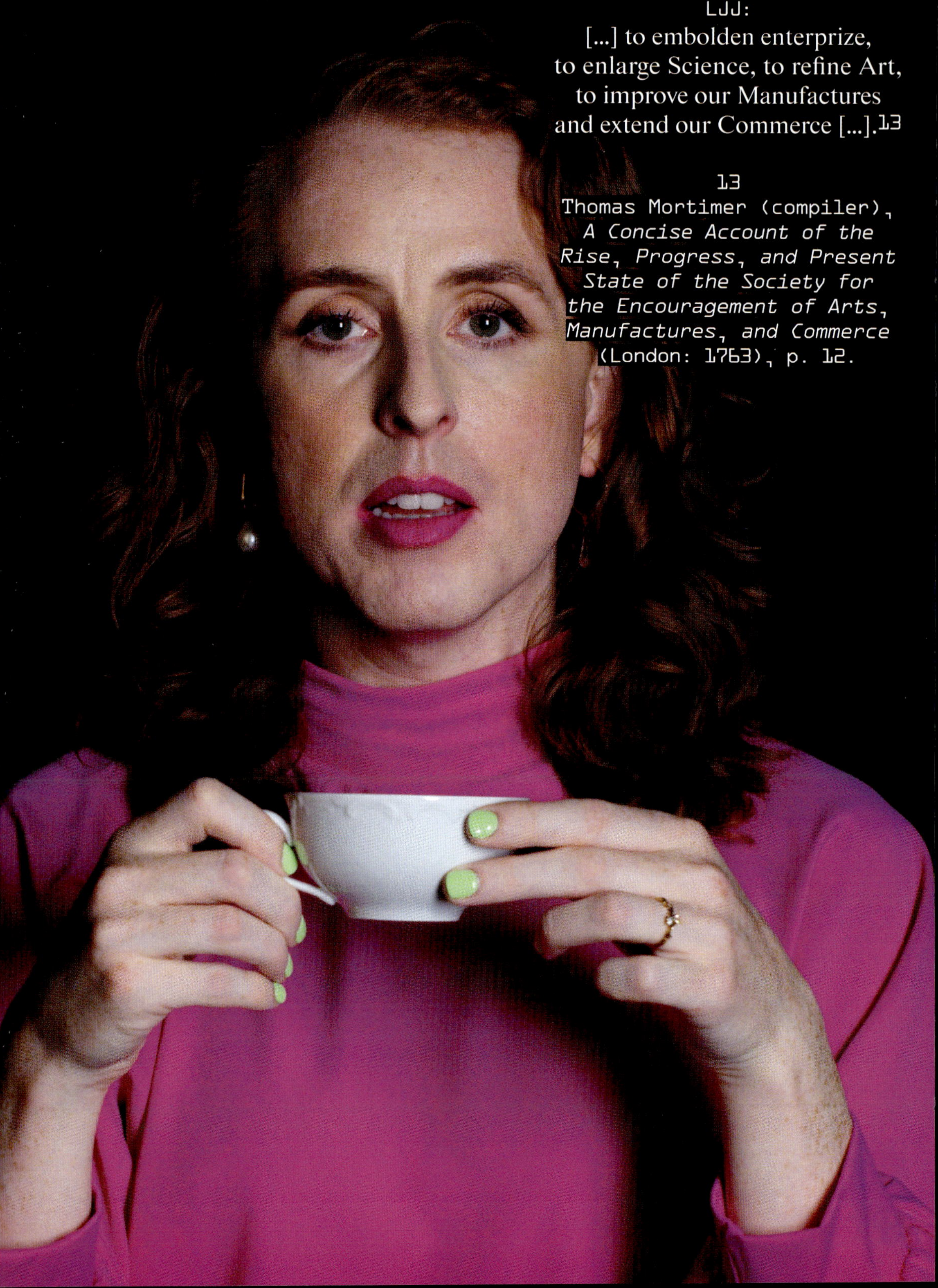
LJJ:
[...] to embolden enterprize,
to enlarge Science, to refine Art,
to improve our Manufactures
and extend our Commerce [...].13

13
Thomas Mortimer (compiler),
A Concise Account of the
Rise, Progress, and Present
State of the Society for
the Encouragement of Arts,
Manufactures, and Commerce
(London: 1763), p. 12.

est. Model of a Wind Mill &c Addo: read 1. Time   21.

d for sowing Land with Acorns &c _   21.

d 1. Time - - - - - - - - -

elating to *Polite Arts & Colonies & Trade*   22.

d - - - - - - - - - -

elating to the Polite Arts & Colonies postponed   25.

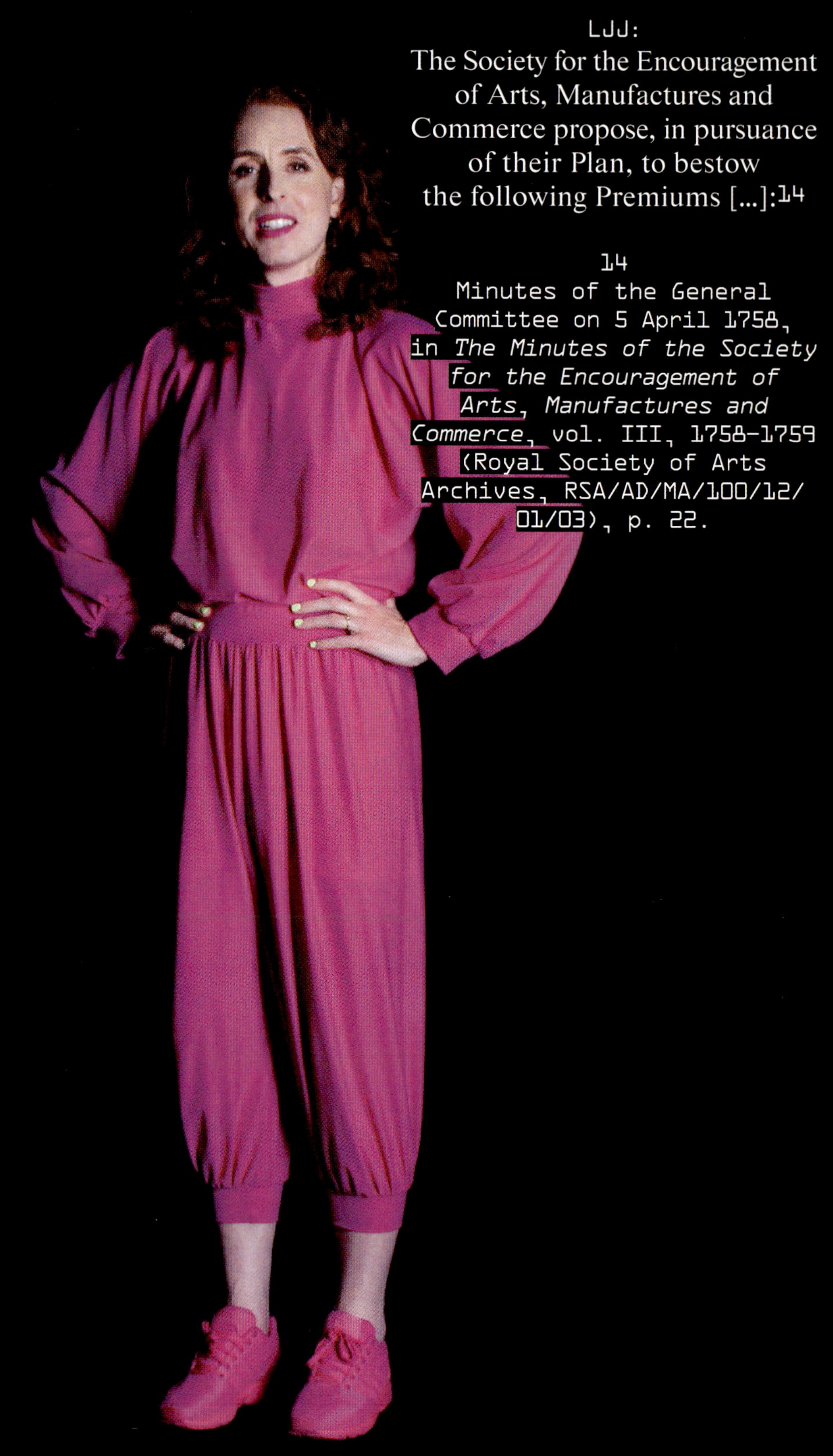
LJJ:
The Society for the Encouragement
of Arts, Manufactures and
Commerce propose, in pursuance
of their Plan, to bestow
the following Premiums [...]:14

14
Minutes of the General
Committee on 5 April 1758,
in *The Minutes of the Society
for the Encouragement of
Arts, Manufactures and
Commerce*, vol. III, 1758–1759
(Royal Society of Arts
Archives, RSA/AD/MA/100/12/
01/03), p. 22.

Premiums for the Advantage of the British Colonies

LJJ:
Premiums for Discoveries
and Improvements in Chymistry,
Dying, Mineralogy, &c.

There will be given for
planting and raising the largest
and best Roots of Madder [...]:
£20.15 [...] [For] Salt-Peter,
a principal Ingredient in Gun
Powder, being purchased
by us in Foreign Parts, at the
Expence of large Sums
of Money [...], whilst great
Quantities are made in France
and other Countries in Europe,
and there being no Doubt
that this most useful Commodity
may also be made in England:
[...] Hereby the person who
shall produce the first and best
Ten thousand Pounds Weight
of Salt-Peter fit for Gun-powder
will be intitled to £200.16

15
Ibid., p. 24.
16
Ibid., pp. 27-28.

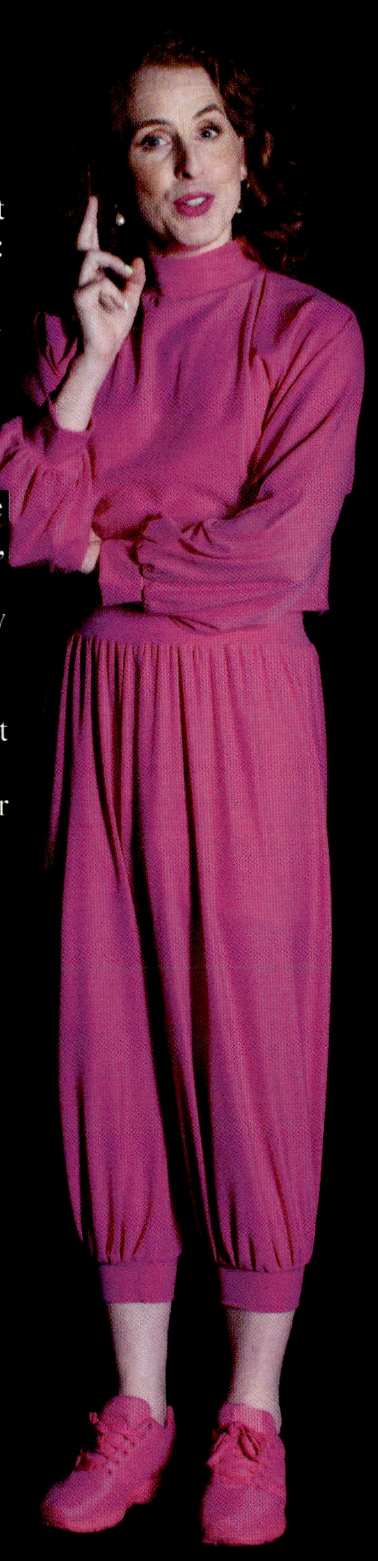

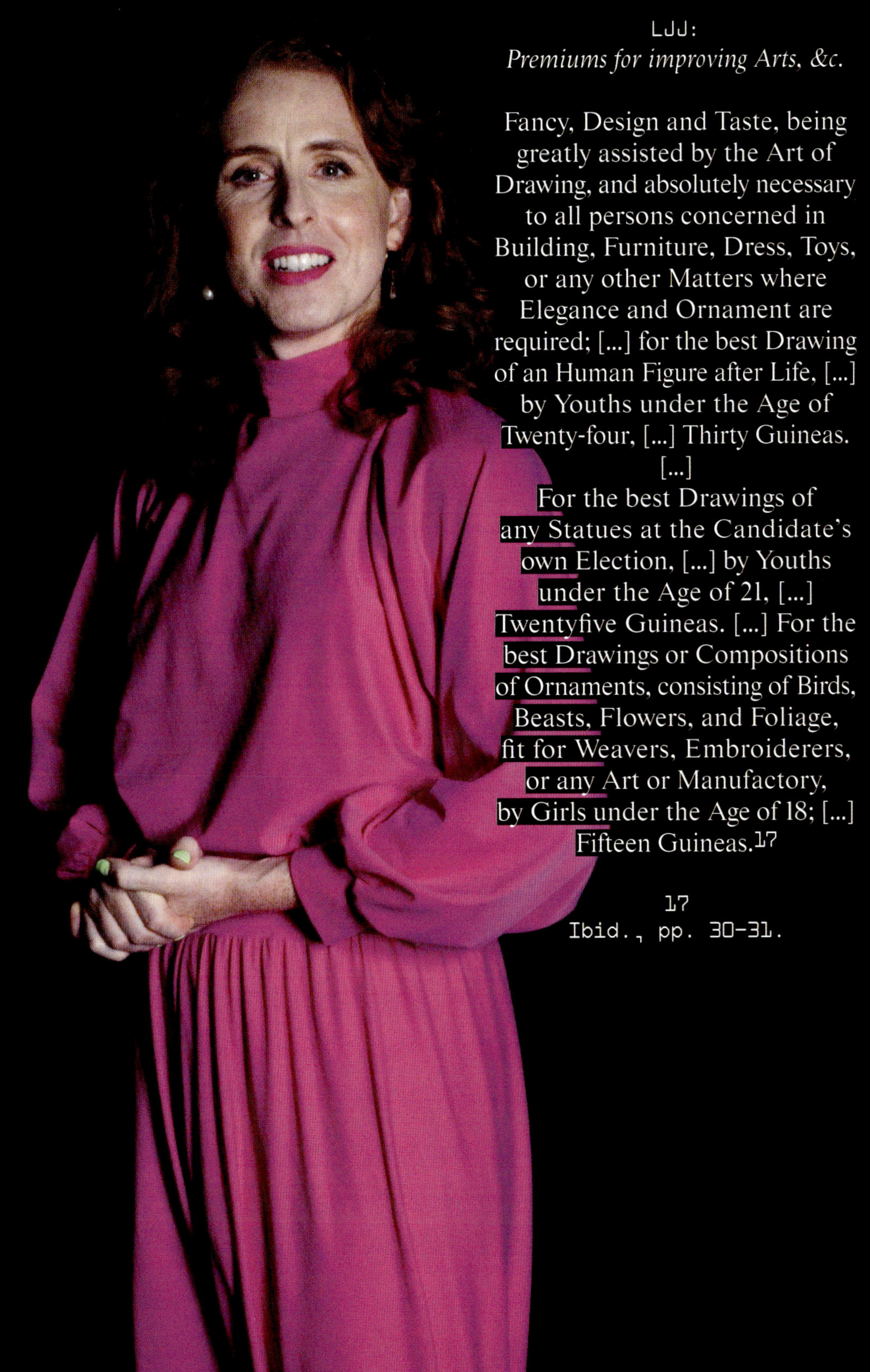
LJJ:
Premiums for improving Arts, &c.

Fancy, Design and Taste, being
greatly assisted by the Art of
Drawing, and absolutely necessary
to all persons concerned in
Building, Furniture, Dress, Toys,
or any other Matters where
Elegance and Ornament are
required; [...] for the best Drawing
of an Human Figure after Life, [...]
by Youths under the Age of
Twenty-four, [...] Thirty Guineas.
[...]
For the best Drawings of
any Statues at the Candidate's
own Election, [...] by Youths
under the Age of 21, [...]
Twentyfive Guineas. [...] For the
best Drawings or Compositions
of Ornaments, consisting of Birds,
Beasts, Flowers, and Foliage,
fit for Weavers, Embroiderers,
or any Art or Manufactory,
by Girls under the Age of 18; [...]
Fifteen Guineas.17

17
Ibid., pp. 30-31.

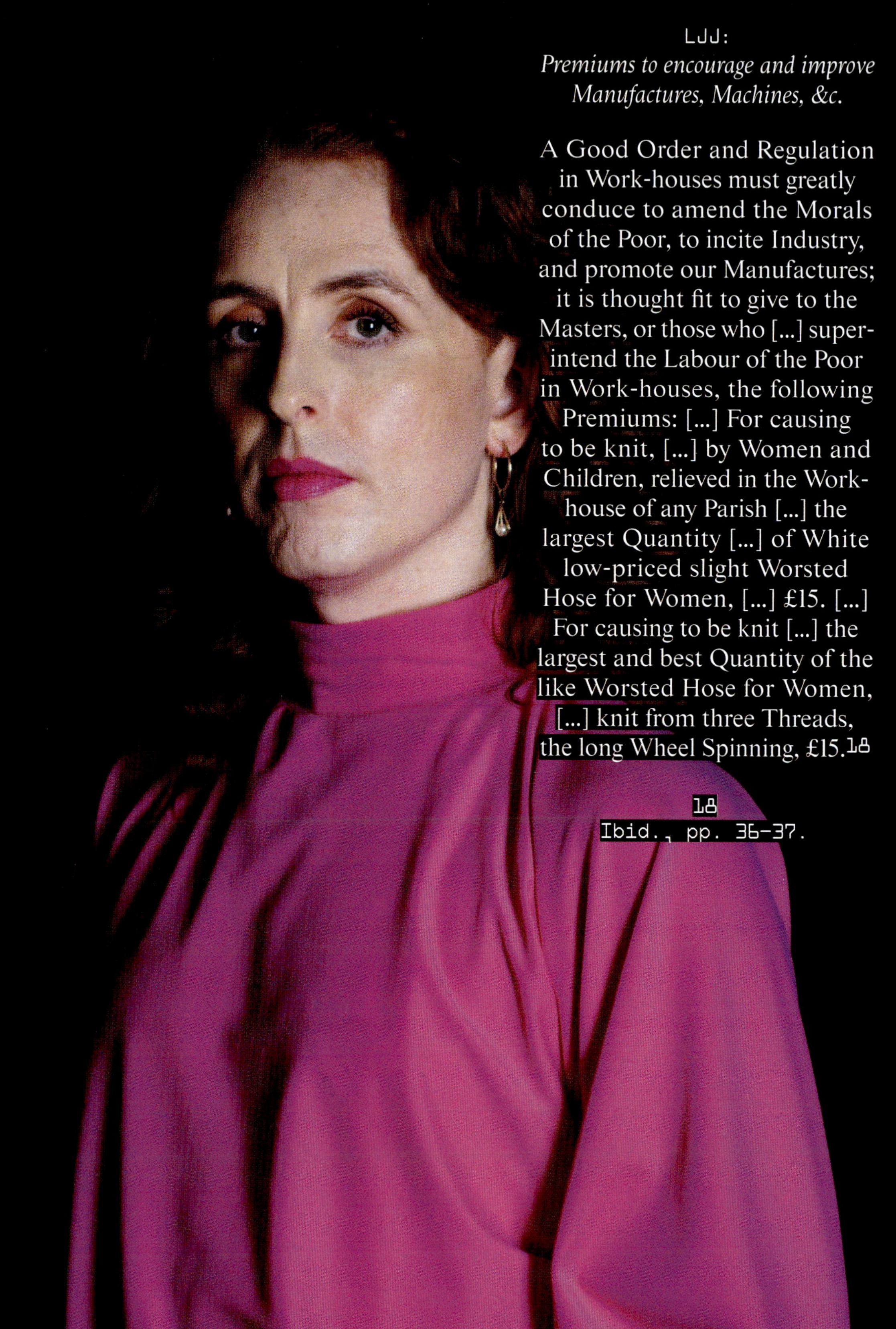

LJJ:
Premiums to encourage and improve Manufactures, Machines, &c.

A Good Order and Regulation in Work-houses must greatly conduce to amend the Morals of the Poor, to incite Industry, and promote our Manufactures; it is thought fit to give to the Masters, or those who [...] super-intend the Labour of the Poor in Work-houses, the following Premiums: [...] For causing to be knit, [...] by Women and Children, relieved in the Work-house of any Parish [...] the largest Quantity [...] of White low-priced slight Worsted Hose for Women, [...] £15. [...] For causing to be knit [...] the largest and best Quantity of the like Worsted Hose for Women, [...] knit from three Threads, the long Wheel Spinning, £15.[18]

18
Ibid., pp. 36–37.

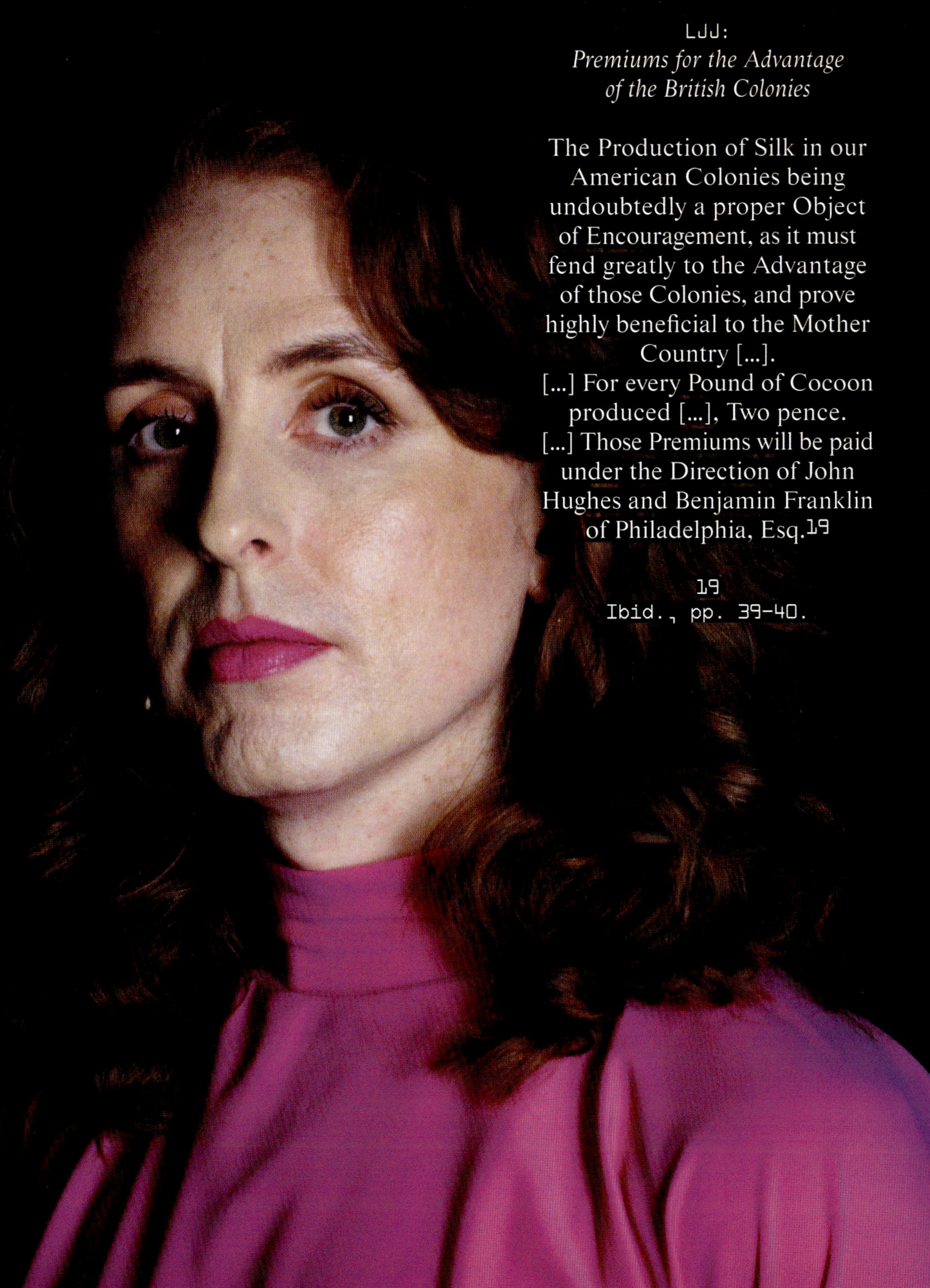

LJJ:
*Premiums for the Advantage
of the British Colonies*

The Production of Silk in our
American Colonies being
undoubtedly a proper Object
of Encouragement, as it must
fend greatly to the Advantage
of those Colonies, and prove
highly beneficial to the Mother
Country [...].
[...] For every Pound of Cocoon
produced [...], Two pence.
[...] Those Premiums will be paid
under the Direction of John
Hughes and Benjamin Franklin
of Philadelphia, Esq.[19]

19
Ibid., pp. 39-40.

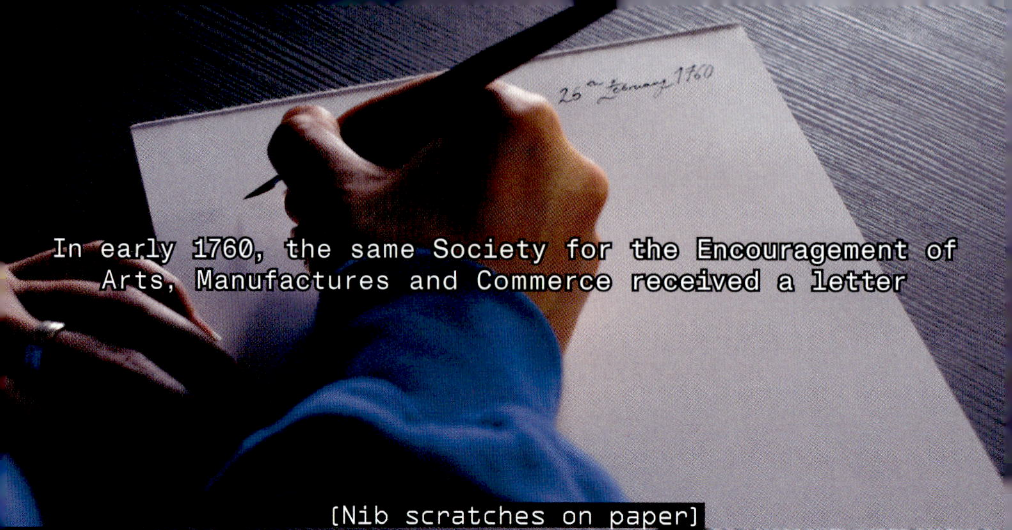

In early 1760, the same Society for the Encouragement of
Arts, Manufactures and Commerce received a letter

[Nib scratches on paper]

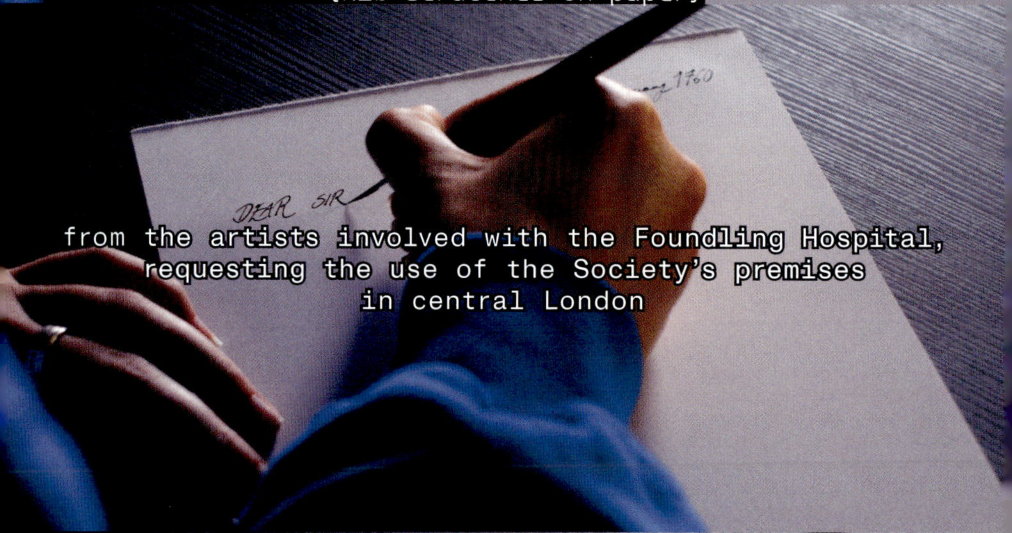

from the artists involved with the Foundling Hospital,
requesting the use of the Society's premises
in central London

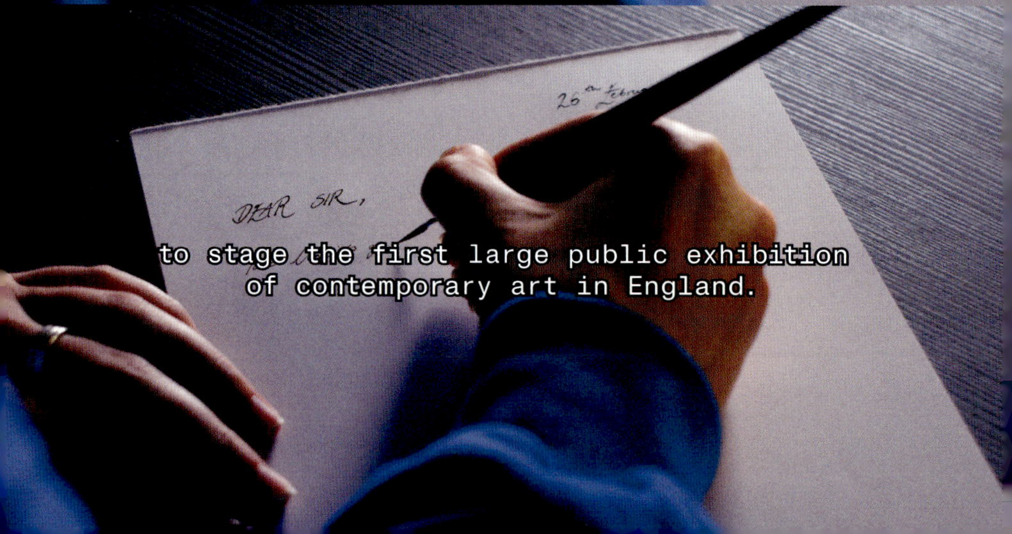

to stage the first large public exhibition
of contemporary art in England.

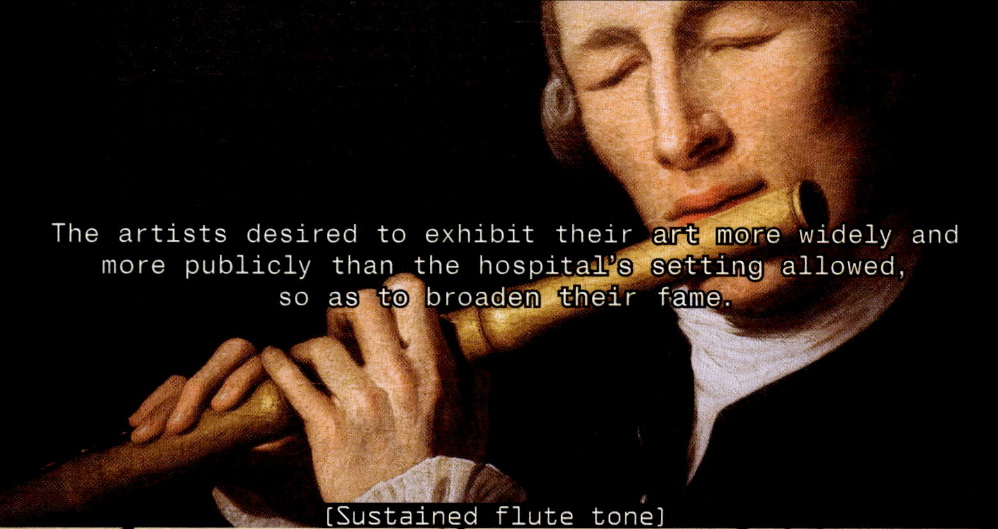

The artists desired to exhibit their art more widely and
more publicly than the hospital's setting allowed,
so as to broaden their fame.

[Sustained flute tone]

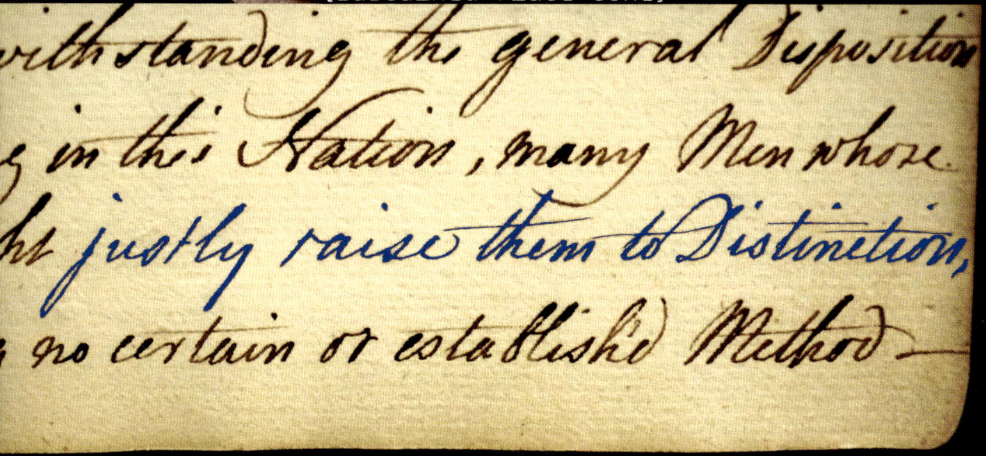

...withstanding the general disposition ...in this Nation, many Men whose ...ht justly raise them to Distinction, ...no certain or establish'd Method—

[Flute gradually fades]

LM:
The Artists of this City [...]
entreat the Society to allow them
the Use of their Room [...].
This Favour they consider as
very important.
[...]

LY:
[T]he Arts will gain Dignity
from the Protection of those
whom the World has already
learned to respect.
[...]

OB:
[T]hat every Painter, Sculptor,
Architect, Engraver, Enchaser,
Seal Cutter and Medallist
should exhibit Once a Year [...].

MK:
A Shilling shall be taken at
the Door, from every One that
enters [...].20

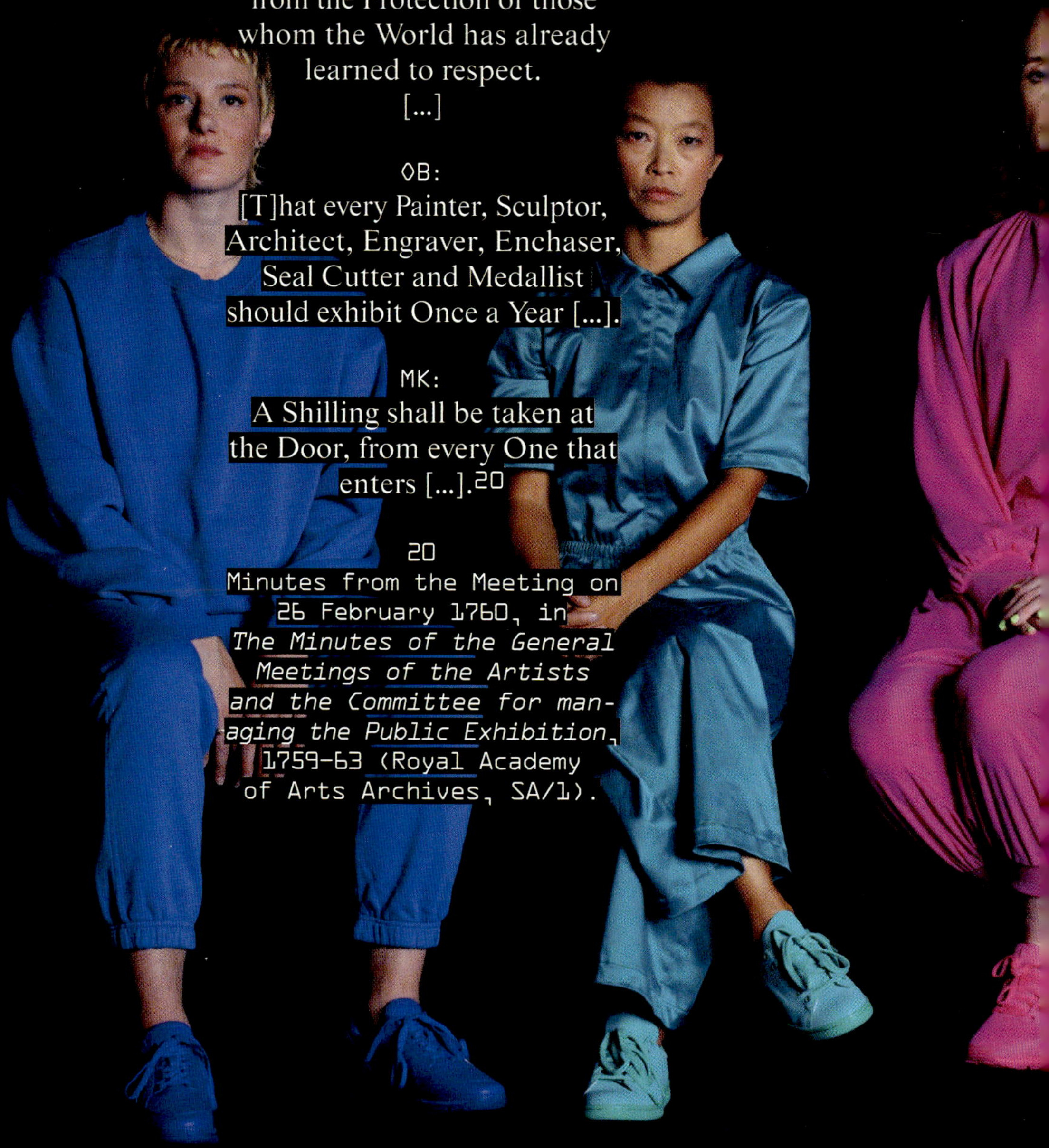

20
Minutes from the Meeting on
26 February 1760, in
The Minutes of the General
Meetings of the Artists
and the Committee for managing the Public Exhibition,
1759–63 (Royal Academy
of Arts Archives, SA/1).

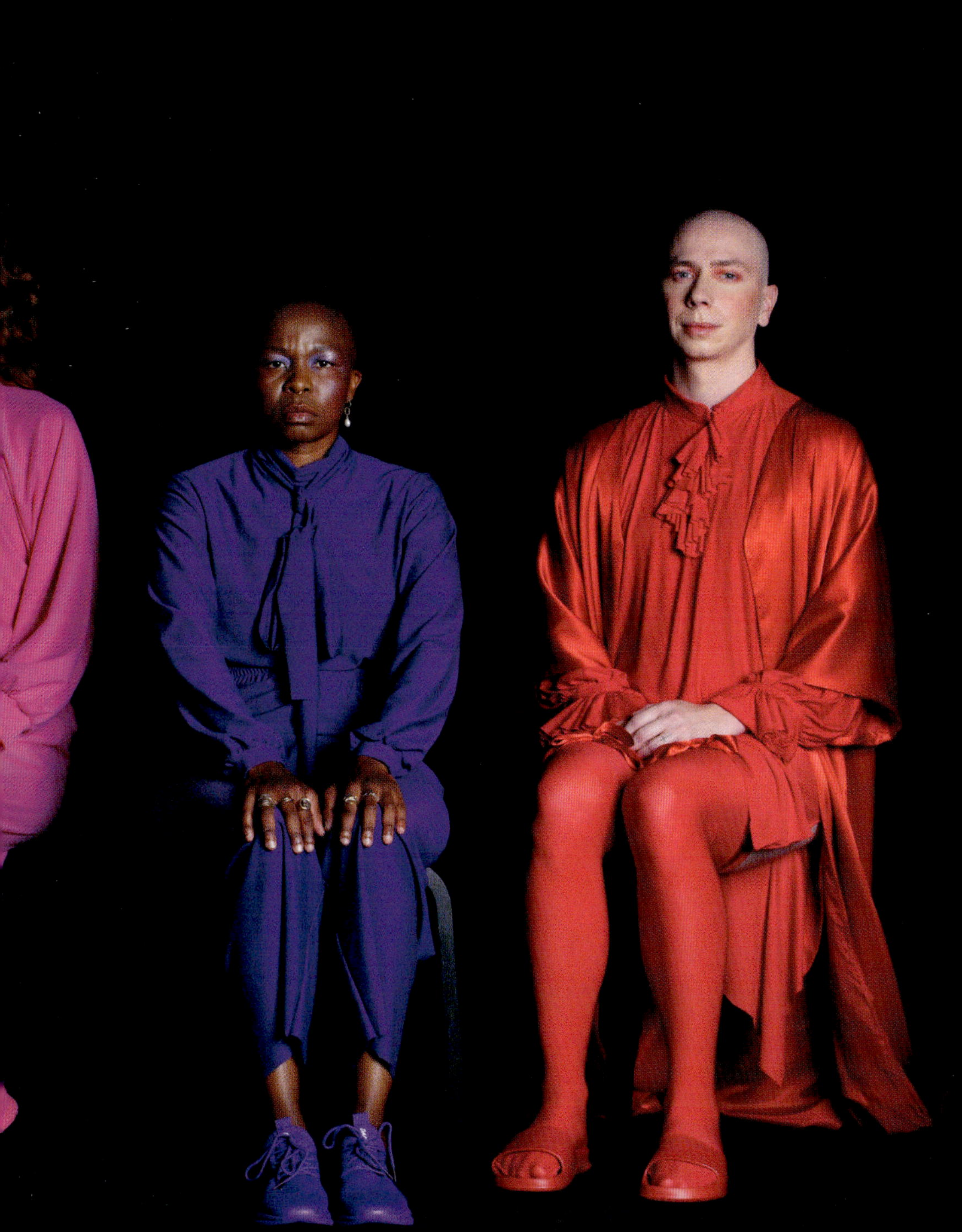

also received.

That no Production be received except the Name of the
be sent therewith.

That the Exhibition be free and open for the Public at
proper Hours & under proper Regulations

Adjourned Sine Die

would indeed attract a wide range of visitors
from all classes,

a prospect that led the Society to appoint
a subcommittee, who decided:

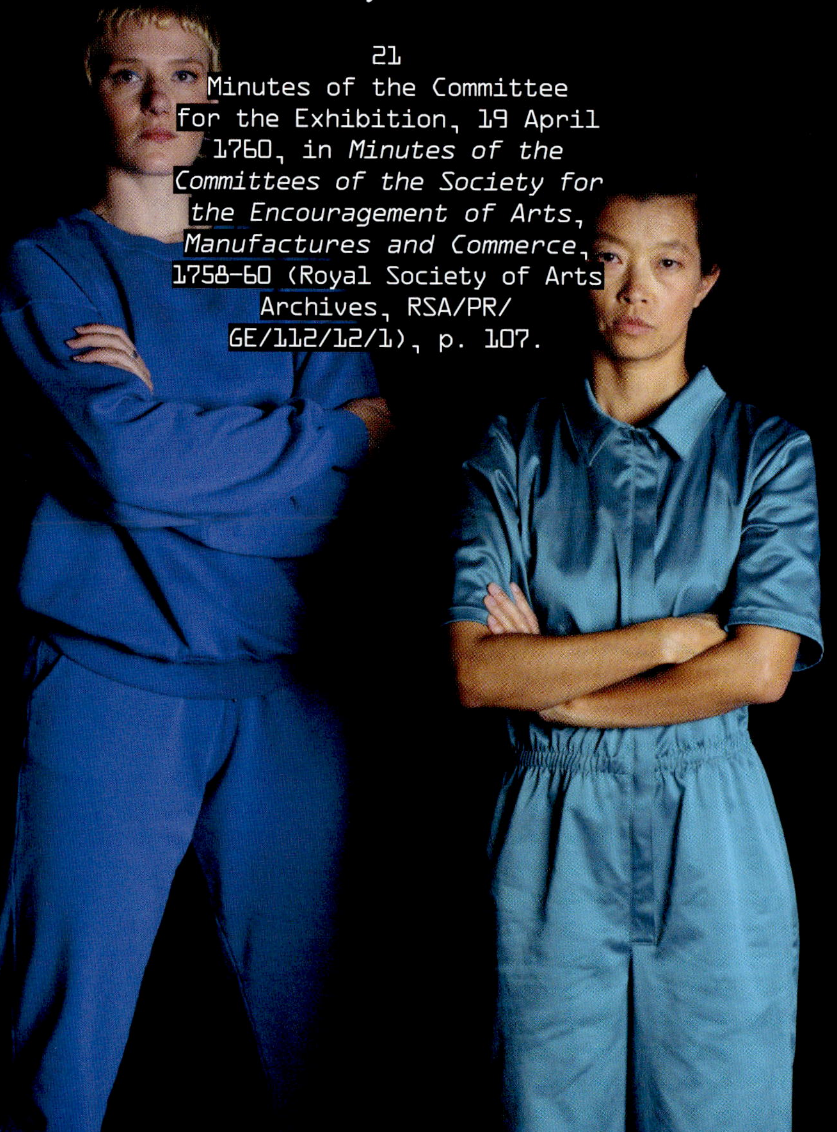

LJJ:
That a Discretionary Power be
lodged in the Officers of the
Society, or whom they shall authorize, to exclude all persons
whom they shall think improper
to be admitted, such as Livery
Servants, foot Soldiers, Porters,
Women with Children &c.
And to prevent all disorders in
the Room, such as Smoaking,
Drinking, &c by turning
the Disorderly Persons out.[21]

21
Minutes of the Committee
for the Exhibition, 19 April
1760, in *Minutes of the
Committees of the Society for
the Encouragement of Arts,
Manufactures and Commerce,
1758–60* (Royal Society of Arts
Archives, RSA/PR/
GE/112/12/1), p. 107.

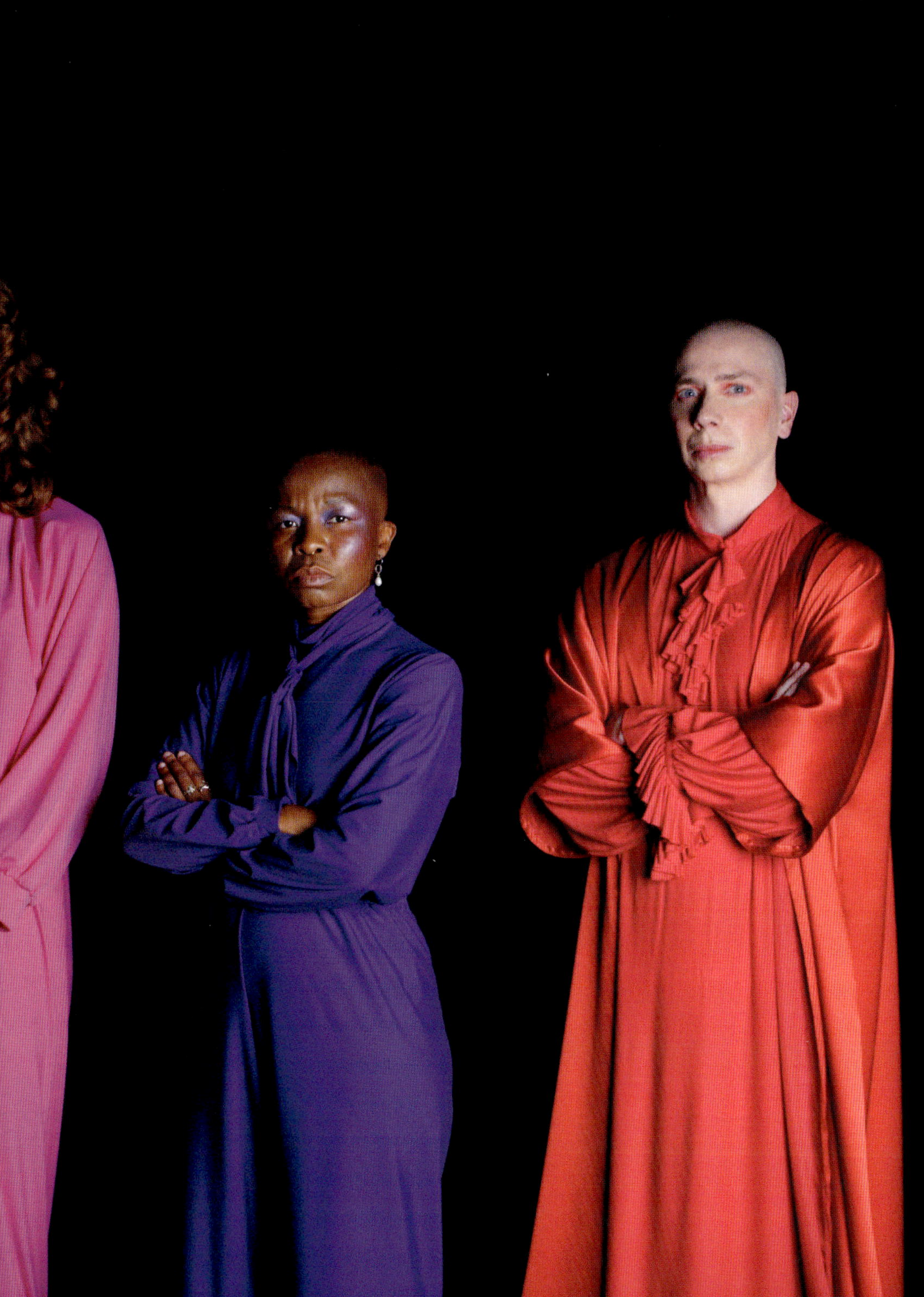

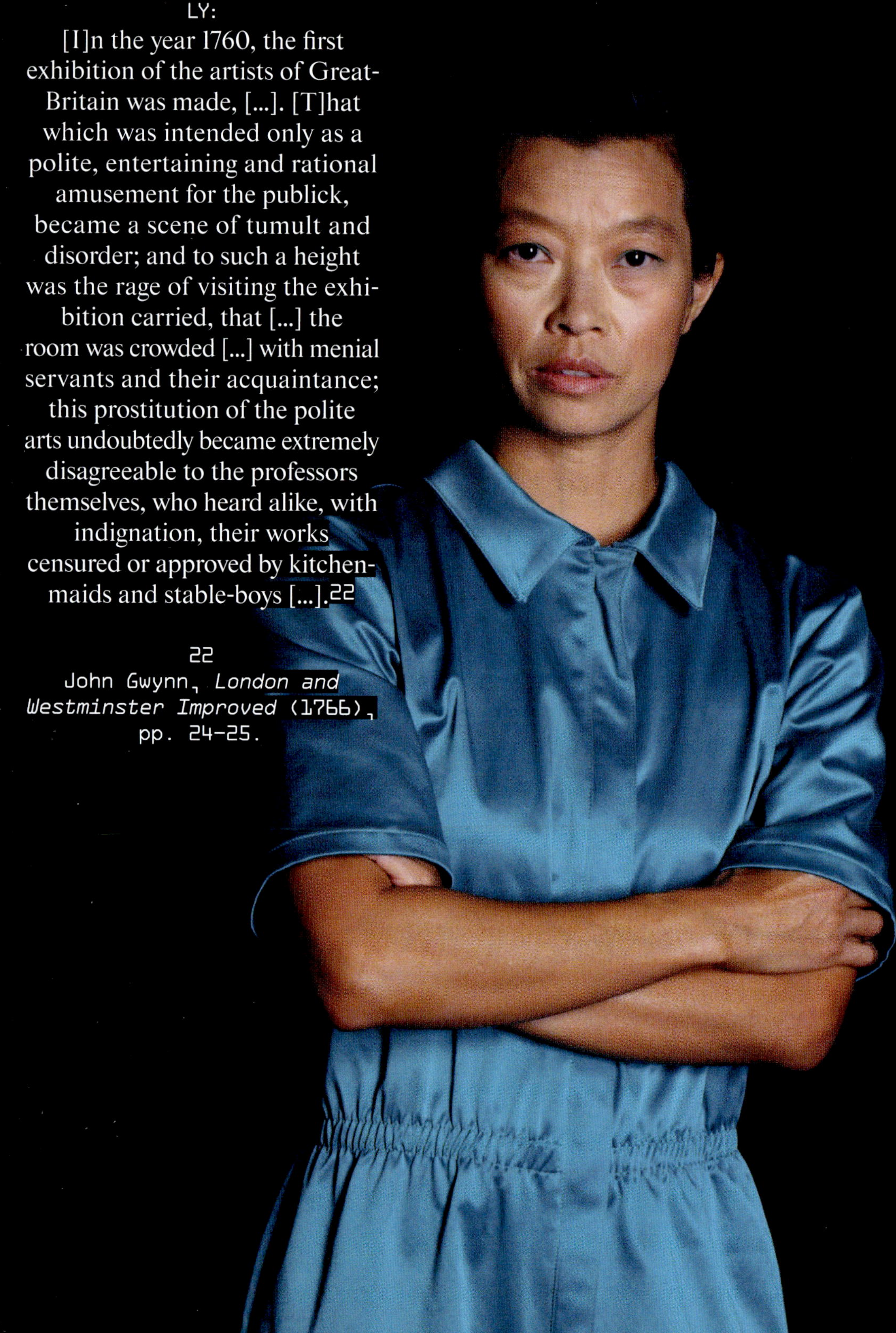
LY:
[I]n the year 1760, the first
exhibition of the artists of Great-
Britain was made, [...]. [T]hat
which was intended only as a
polite, entertaining and rational
amusement for the publick,
became a scene of tumult and
disorder; and to such a height
was the rage of visiting the exhibition carried, that [...] the
room was crowded [...] with menial
servants and their acquaintance;
this prostitution of the polite
arts undoubtedly became extremely
disagreeable to the professors
themselves, who heard alike, with
indignation, their works
censured or approved by kitchen-
maids and stable-boys [...].22

22
John Gwynn, London and
Westminster Improved (1766),
pp. 24-25.

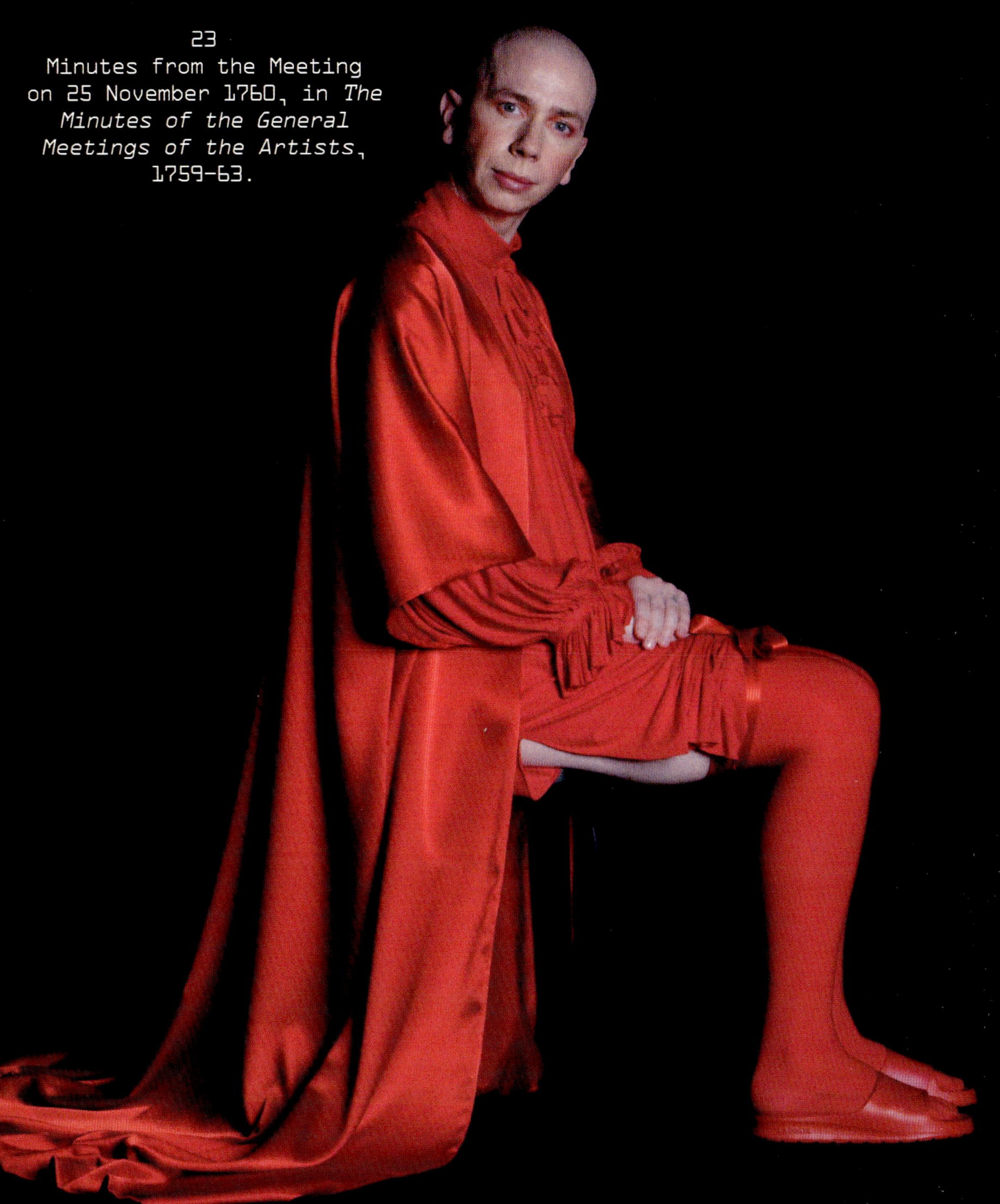
OB:
Great Inconvenience having
been found by Inferior People
crowding last Year.23

23
Minutes from the Meeting
on 25 November 1760, in *The
Minutes of the General
Meetings of the Artists,
1759-63*.

MK:
The Exhibition of last Year
was crowded and incommoded
by the intrusion of great
Numbers whose Stations and
education made them no
proper Judges of Statuary and
Painting, and who were
made idle and tumultuous by
the opportunity of a shew.

LM:
It is therefore intended that
the Catalogues shall be sold for
a shilling each, and none
allowed to enter without
a Catalogue which may serve
as a ticket for admission.24

24
Minutes from the Meeting
on 8 December 1760, in The
Minutes of the General
Meetings of the Artists,
1759-63.

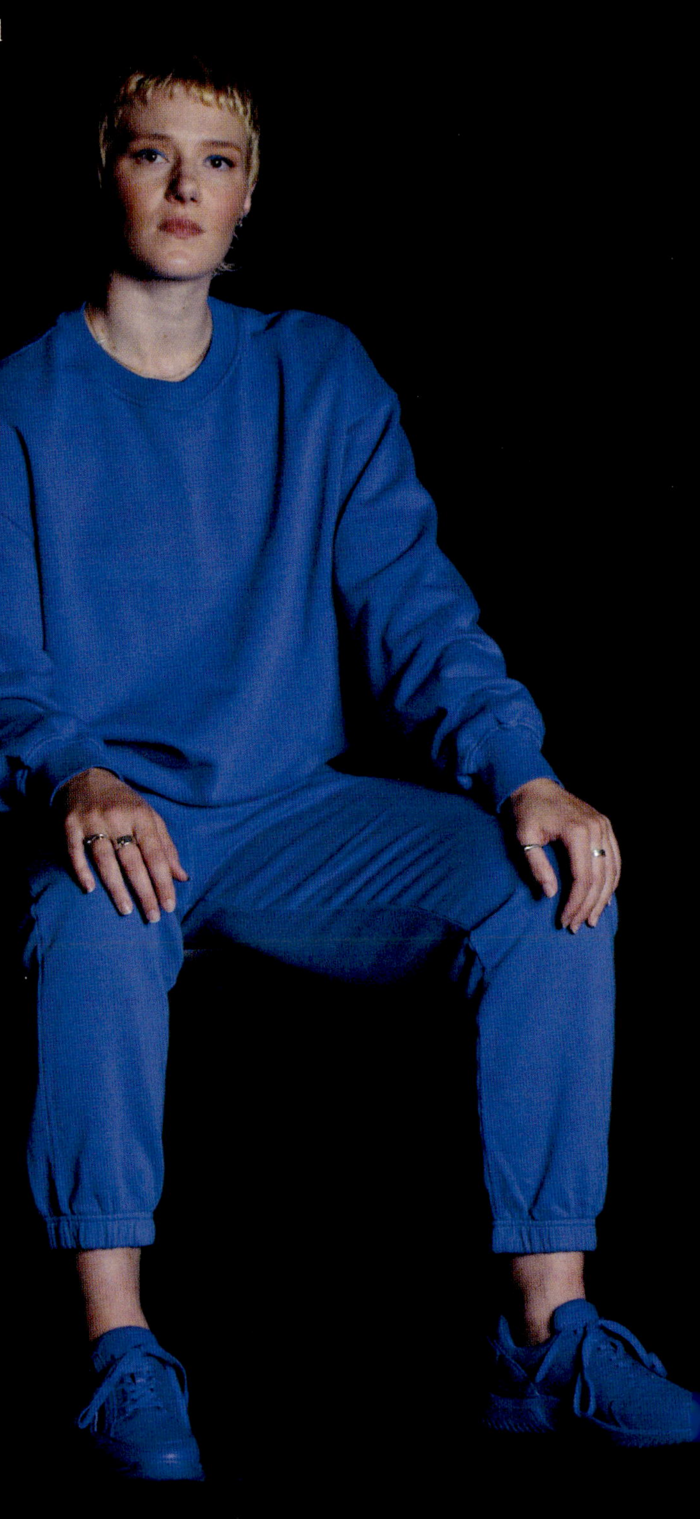

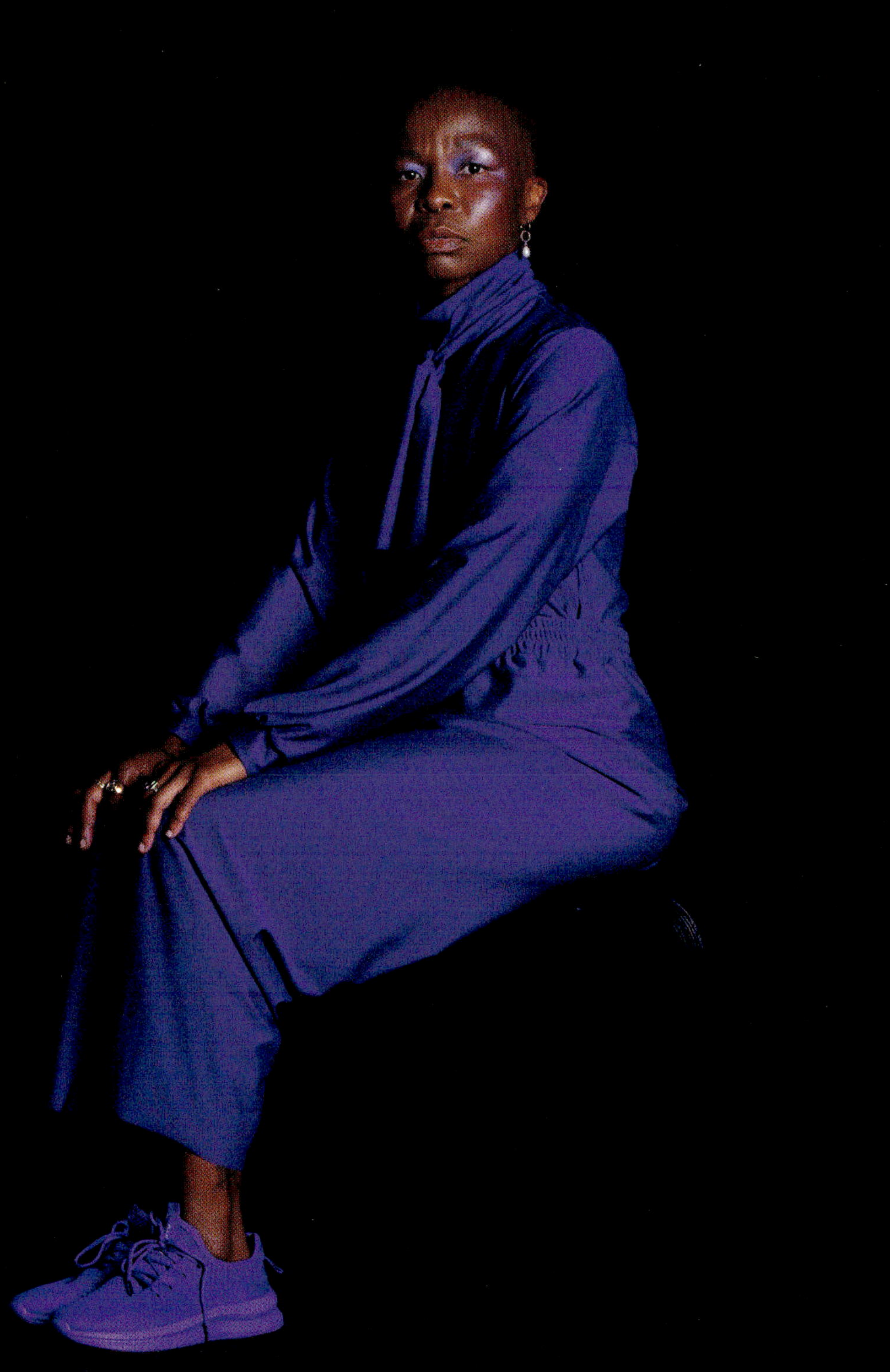

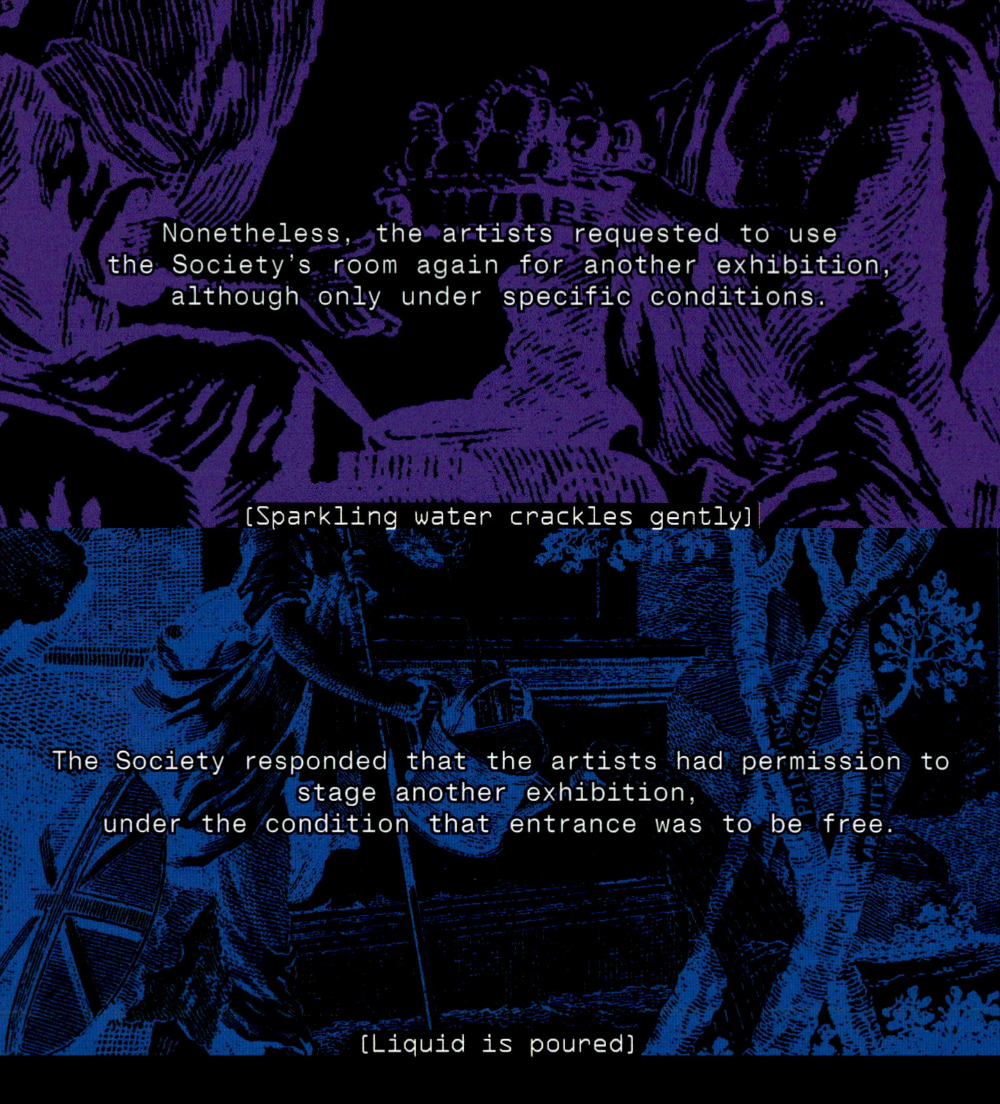
Nonetheless, the artists requested to use
the Society's room again for another exhibition,
although only under specific conditions.

[Sparkling water crackles gently]

The Society responded that the artists had permission to
stage another exhibition,
under the condition that entrance was to be free.

[Liquid is poured]

That the Exhibition be free and open for the Public

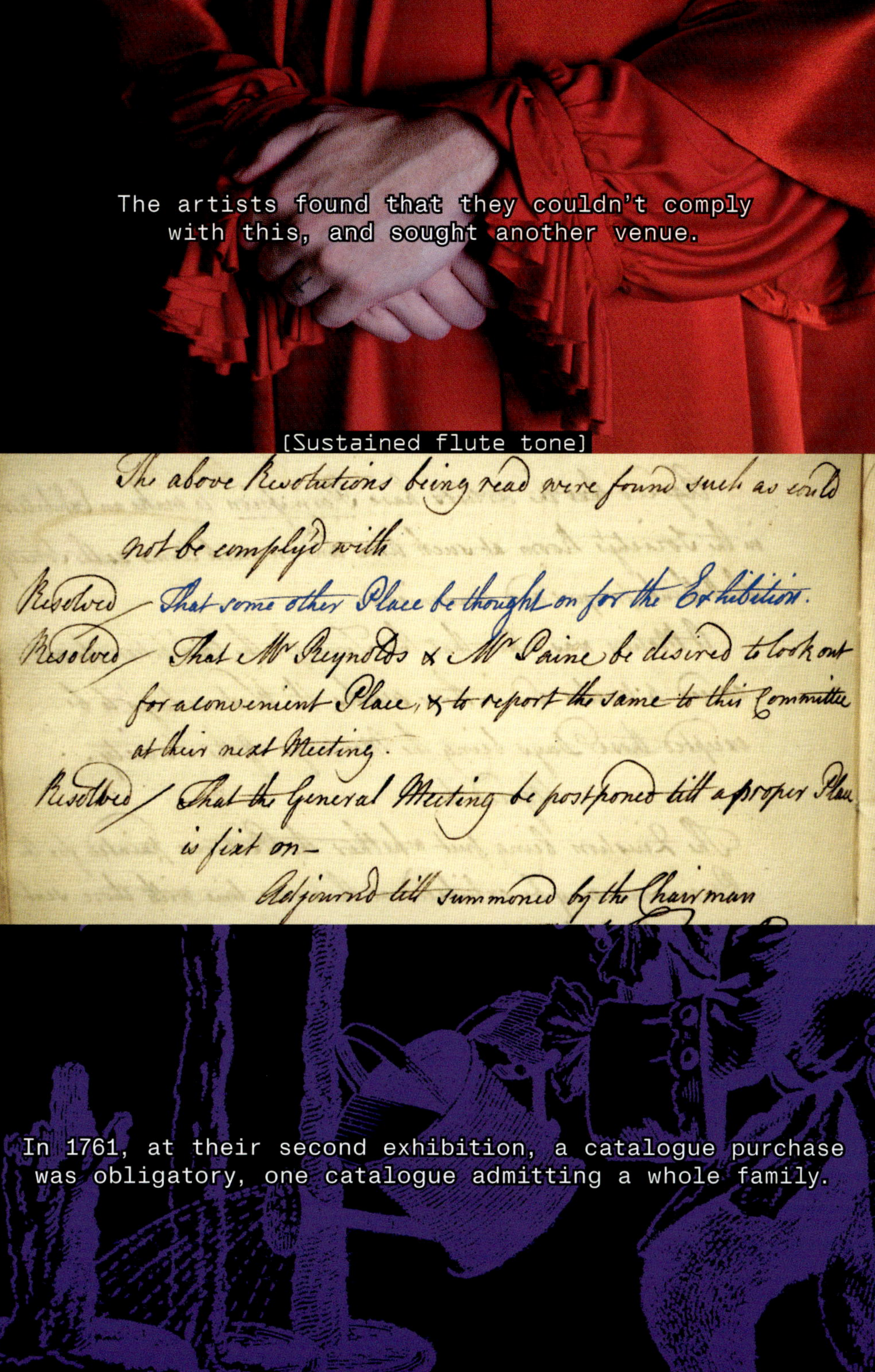

The above Resolutions being read were found such as could
not be comply'd with
Resolved — That some other Place be thought on for the Exhibition.
Resolved — That Mr Reynolds & Mr Paine be desired to look out
for a convenient Place, & to report the same to this Committee
at their next Meeting.
Resolved / That the General Meeting be postponed till a proper Place
is fixt on —
                        Adjourned till summoned by the Chairman

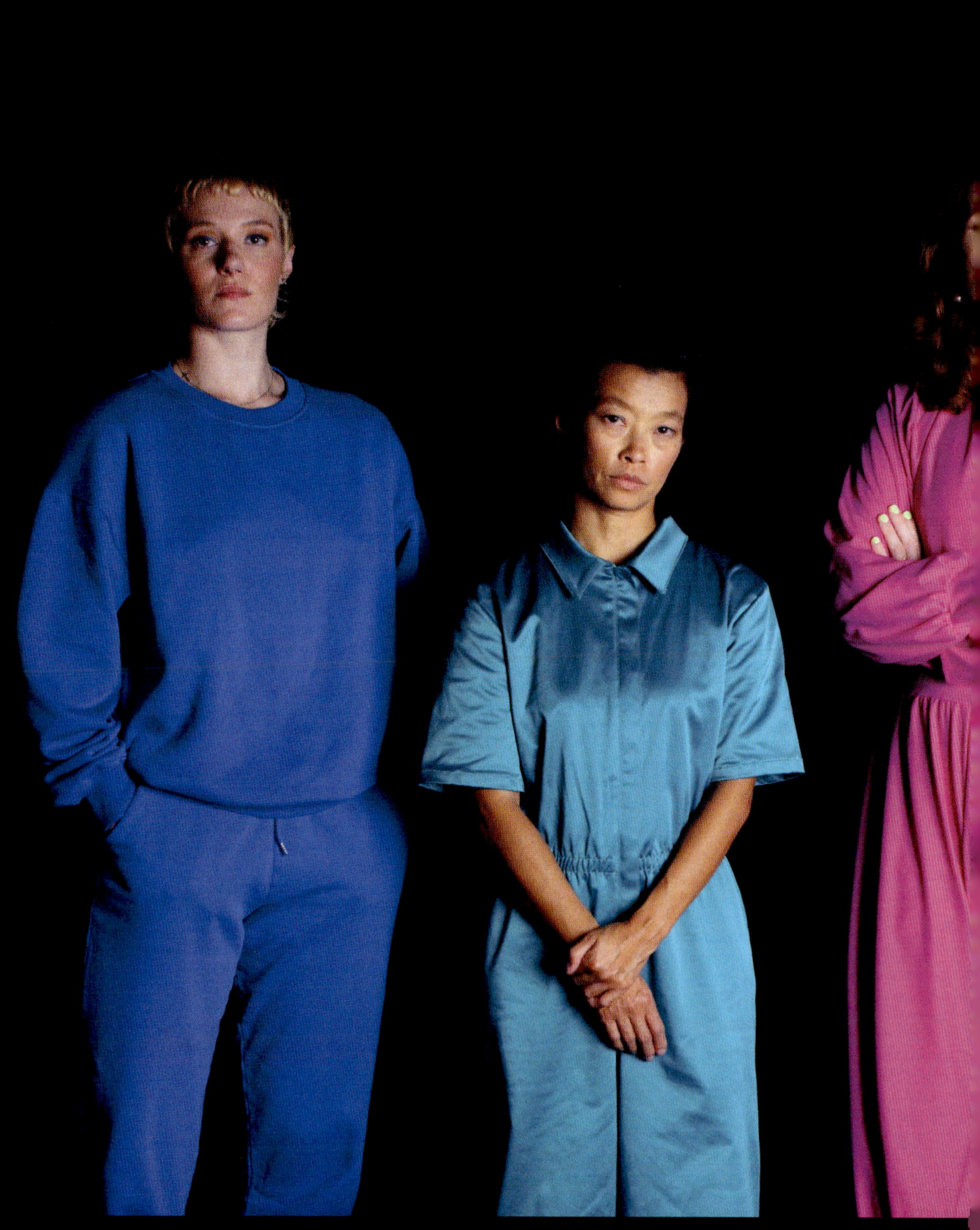

But this mode of admission was
still productive of crowd and
disorder, and it was therefore
altered the next year.[25]

25
Edward Edwards, *Anecdotes of
Painters, Who Have Resided or
Been Born in England: With
Critical Remarks on Their
Productions* (London: Leigh and
Sotheby, 1808), p. xxvi.

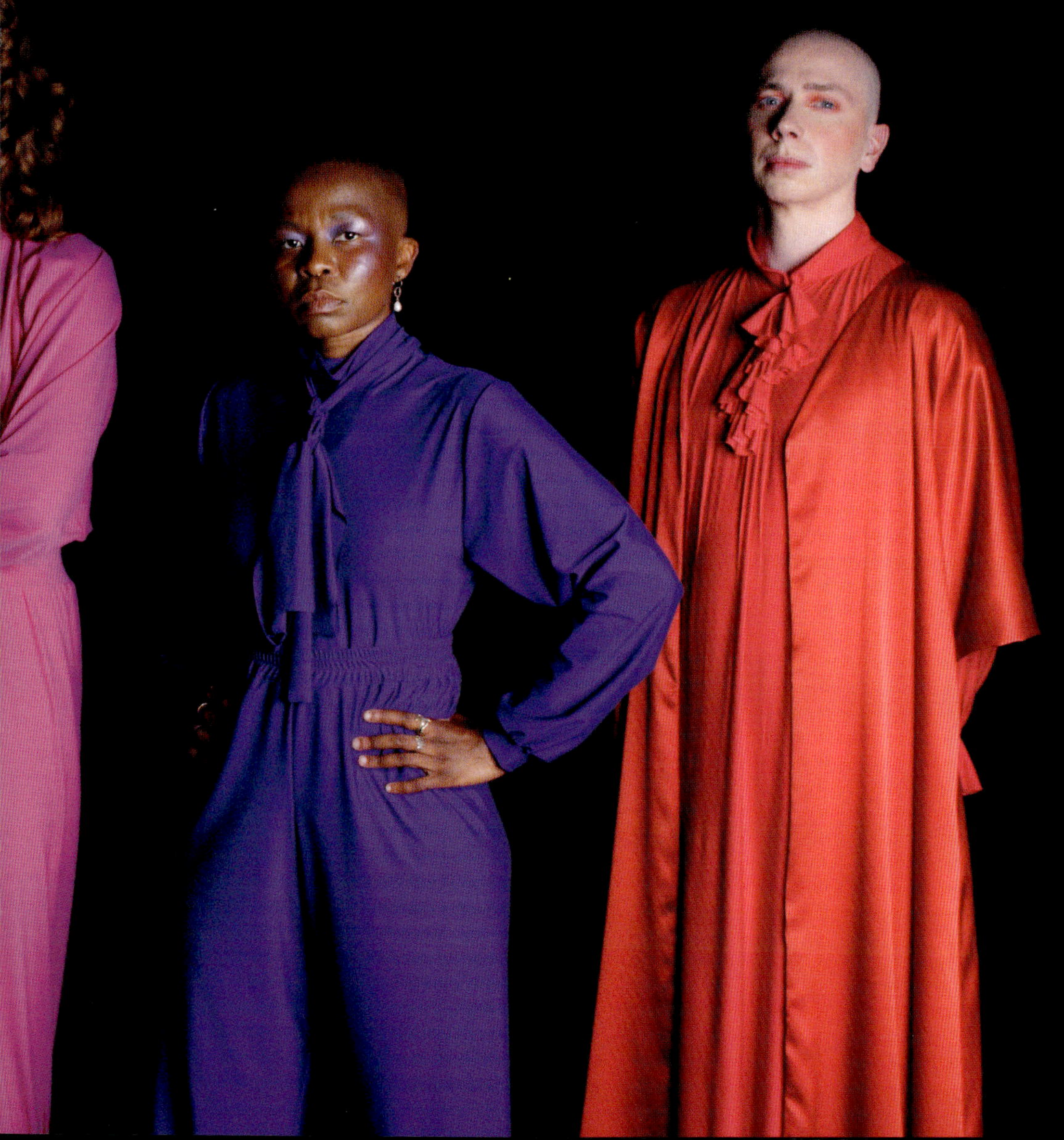

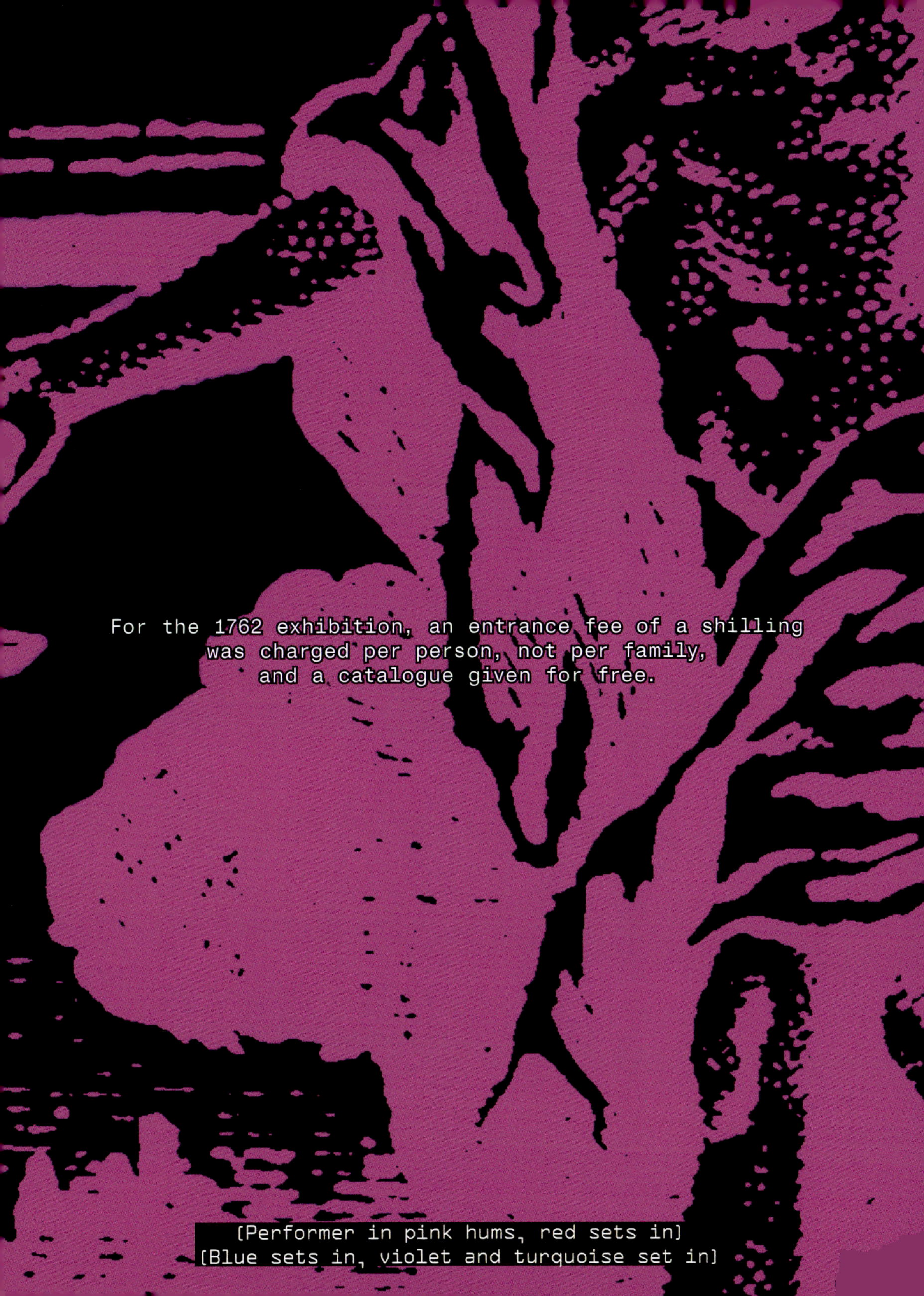
For the 1762 exhibition, an entrance fee of a shilling
was charged per person, not per family,
and a catalogue given for free.

[Performer in pink hums, red sets in]
[Blue sets in, violet and turquoise set in]

A CATALOGUE

of the

Pictures, Sculptures, Models, Drawings, Prints, &c.

Exhibited by the

SOCIETY of ARTISTS

of

Great — Britain,

AT THE

Great Room, in spring Gardens, Charing Cross.

May the 17th, Anno 1762.

Being the Third Year of their Exhibition.

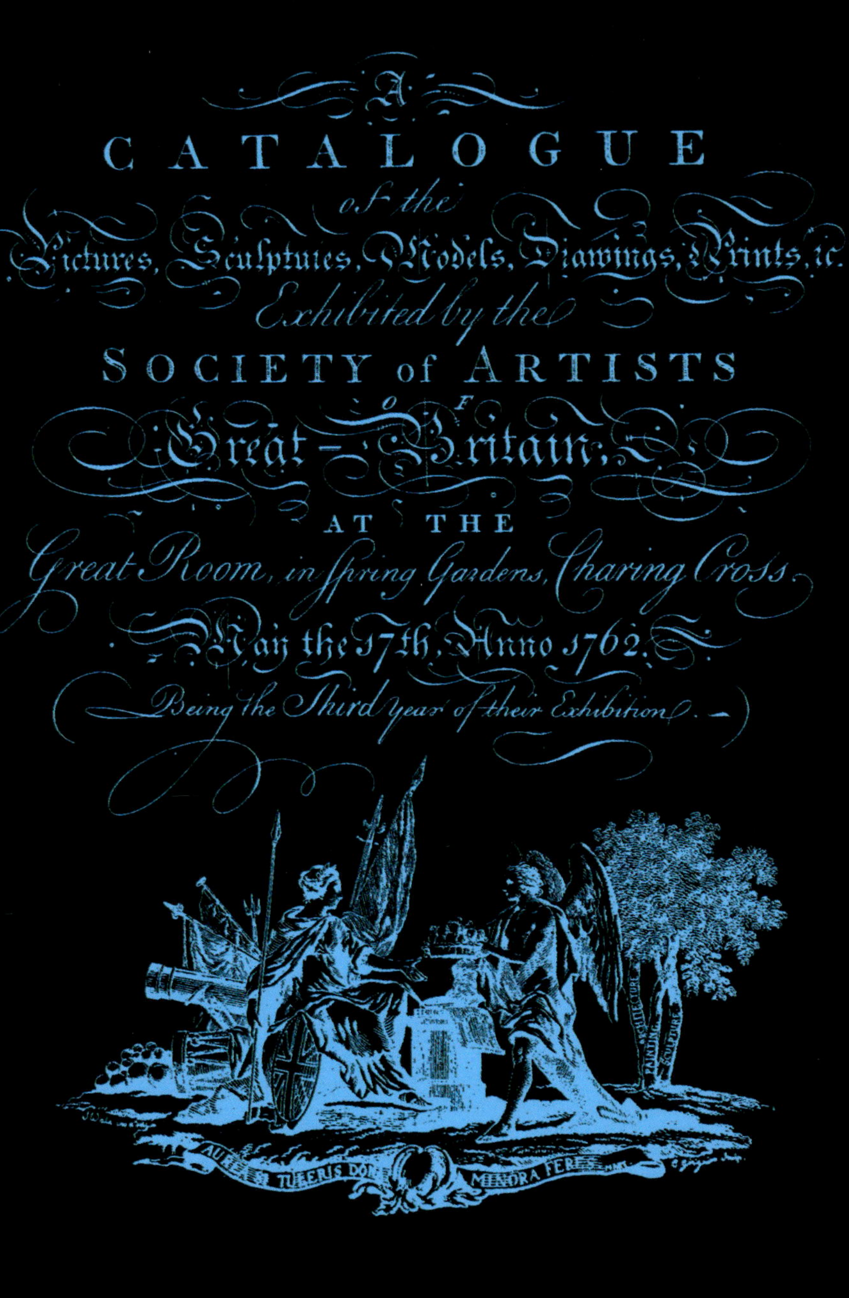

[3]

PREFACE.

MK:
Of the price put upon this
Exhibition some account may
be demanded.

LY:
Whoever sets his work to be
shewn, naturally desires a
multitude of spectators, but his
desire defeats its own end, when
spectators assemble in such
numbers as to obstruct one
another.

OB:
Tho' we are far from wishing
to diminish the pleasures, or
depreciate the sentiments of any
class of the community, we
know however, what every one
knows, that all cannot be judges
or purchasers of works of art;
yet we have already found by
experience, that all are desirous
to see an exhibition.

LM:
When the terms of admission
were low, our room was throng'd
with such multitudes as made
access dangerous, and frightened
away those, whose approbation
was most desired.26

26
A Catalogue of the Pictures,
Sculptures, Models, Drawings,
Prints, &c. Exhibited by the
Society of Artists of Great-
Britain, at the Great Room in
Spring Gardens, Charing-Cross,
May 17th Anno 1762 (London:
1762), p. v.

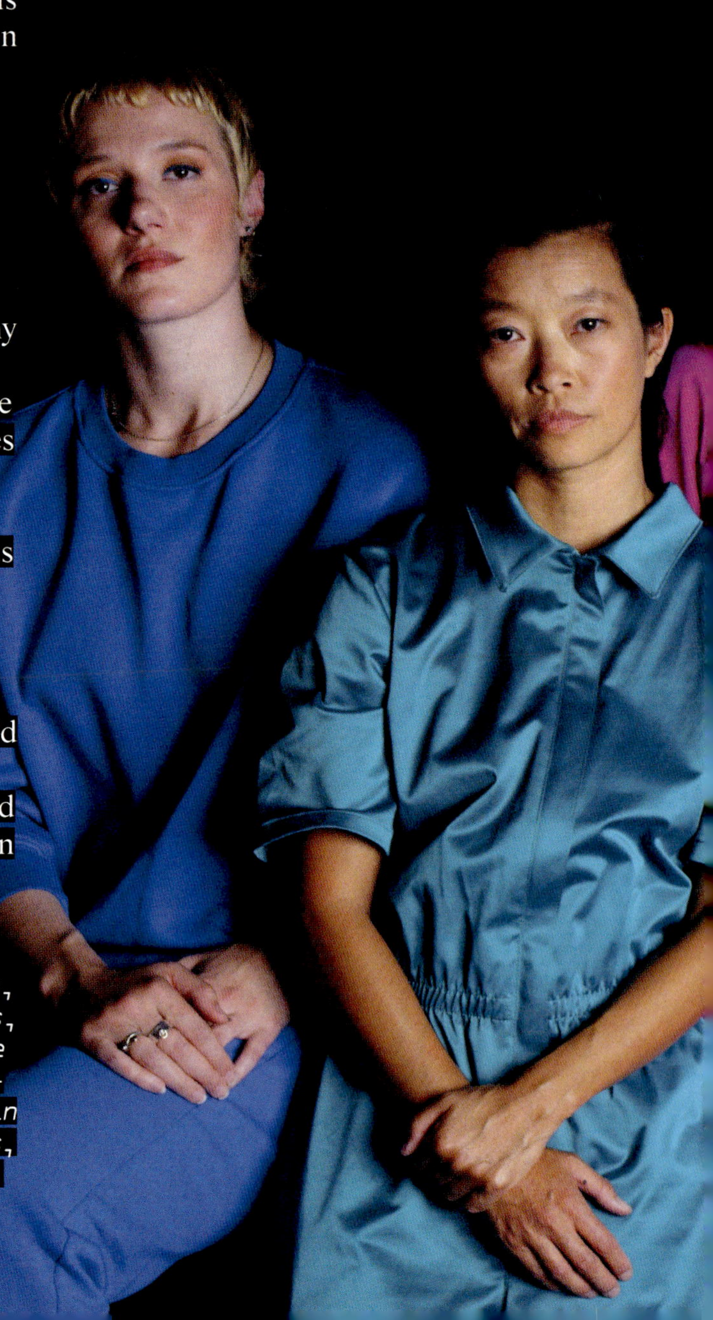

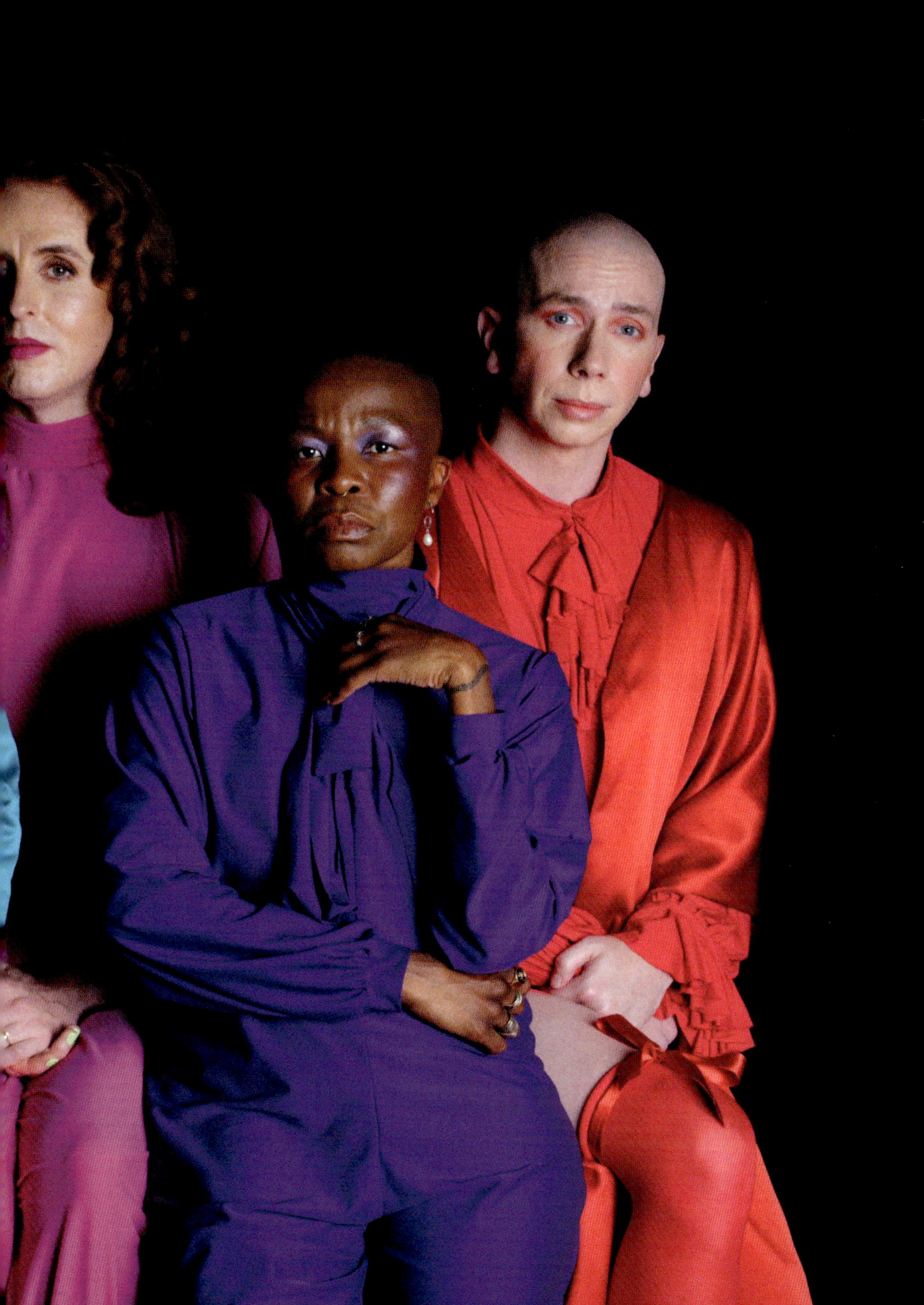

OF THE STANDARD OF TASTE.

BY

DAVID HUME, Esq;

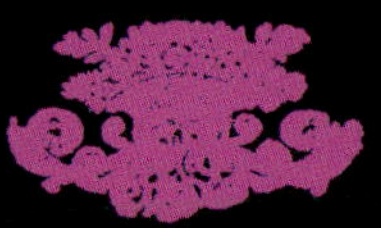

1757

A few great and refined geniuses will
communicate their taste and
knowledge to a whole people, and produce the greatest improvements.[27]
It is very natural for us to seek a
Standard of Taste; a rule, by which the
various sentiments of men may
be reconciled; or at least, a decision
afforded, confirming one sentiment,
and condemning another.[28]
A man, who has had no opportunity
of comparing the different kinds
of beauty, is indeed totally unqualified
to pronounce an opinion with regard
to any object presented to him.[29]
Thus, though the principles of taste be
universal, and nearly, if not entirely
the same in all men; yet few are
qualified to give judgment on any work
of art, or establish their own sentiment
as the standard of beauty.[30]
Though men of delicate taste are rare,
they are easily to be distinguished
in society, by the soundness of their
understanding and the superiority of
their faculties above the rest of
mankind.[31]

[27]
David Hume, 'Of National
Characters', in *Essays and
Treatises on Several Subjects*
(London: A. Millar, 1760), p. 339.
[28]
David Hume, 'Of the Standard
of Taste', in *Four Dissertations*
(London: A. Millar, 1757),
pp. 207–8.
[29]
Ibid., 223.
[30]
Ibid., 228.
[31]
Ibid., 231.

LONDON AND WESTMINSTER IMPROVED,

ILLUSTRATED by PLANS.

By *JOHN GWYNN.*

1766

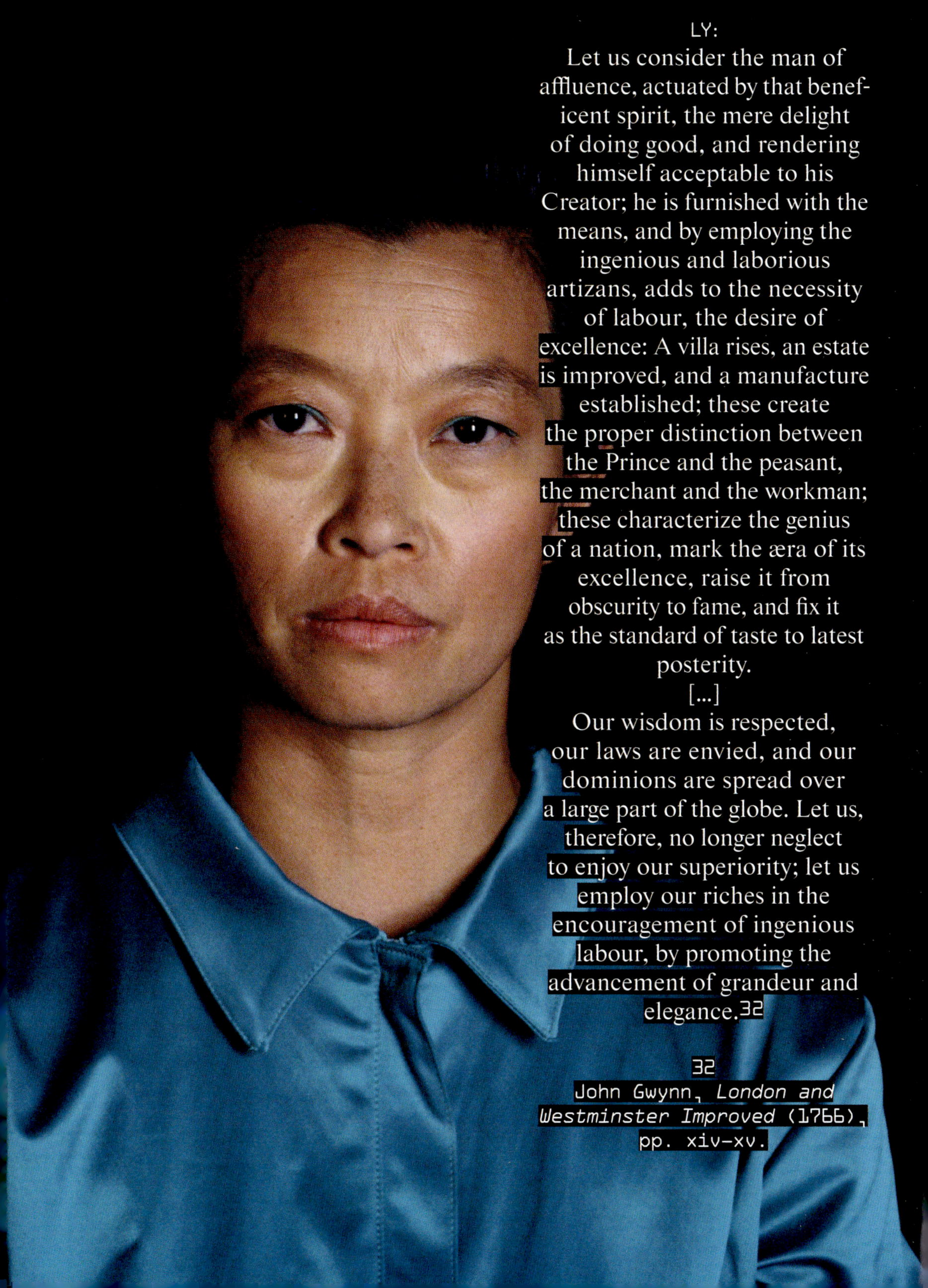

LY:
Let us consider the man of
affluence, actuated by that beneficent spirit, the mere delight
of doing good, and rendering
himself acceptable to his
Creator; he is furnished with the
means, and by employing the
ingenious and laborious
artizans, adds to the necessity
of labour, the desire of
excellence: A villa rises, an estate
is improved, and a manufacture
established; these create
the proper distinction between
the Prince and the peasant,
the merchant and the workman;
these characterize the genius
of a nation, mark the æra of its
excellence, raise it from
obscurity to fame, and fix it
as the standard of taste to latest
posterity.
[…]
Our wisdom is respected,
our laws are envied, and our
dominions are spread over
a large part of the globe. Let us,
therefore, no longer neglect
to enjoy our superiority; let us
employ our riches in the
encouragement of ingenious
labour, by promoting the
advancement of grandeur and
elegance.32

32
John Gwynn, London and
Westminster Improved (1766),
pp. xiv–xv.

LIST OF ILLUSTRATIONS
Cover image & pp. 65–111:
Vika Kirchenbauer, *Compassion and Inconvenience* (2024), video stills, courtesy the artist & VG Bild Kunst

CONTRIBUTOR
Vika Kirchenbauer
PUBLISHING EDITOR
Ilaria Bombelli (Mousse)
EDITORIAL COORDINATOR
Emma Passarella (Mousse)
CONTENT EDITING
Judith Sieber, Tamara Antonijević, Christopher Weickenmeier
COPY EDITING / PROOFREADING
Nancy Chapple, Rosie Heinrich
GRAPHIC DESIGN
Anna Azzali (Mousse)

FUNDED BY
Hochschule für Bildende Künste Braunschweig

PUBLISHED AND DISTRIBUTED BY
Mousse Publishing
Contrappunto s.r.l.
via Pier Candido Decembrio 28,
20137, Milan–Italy

AVAILABLE THROUGH
Mousse Publishing, Milan
moussemagazine.it

FIRST EDITION 2025

PRINTED IN ITALY BY
Arti Grafiche Parini

ISBN 978-88-6749-685-3

€ 25 / $ 30

Braunschweig University of Art
Hochschule für Bildende Künste Braunschweig